W9-BLR-690

BIO*luminescence*

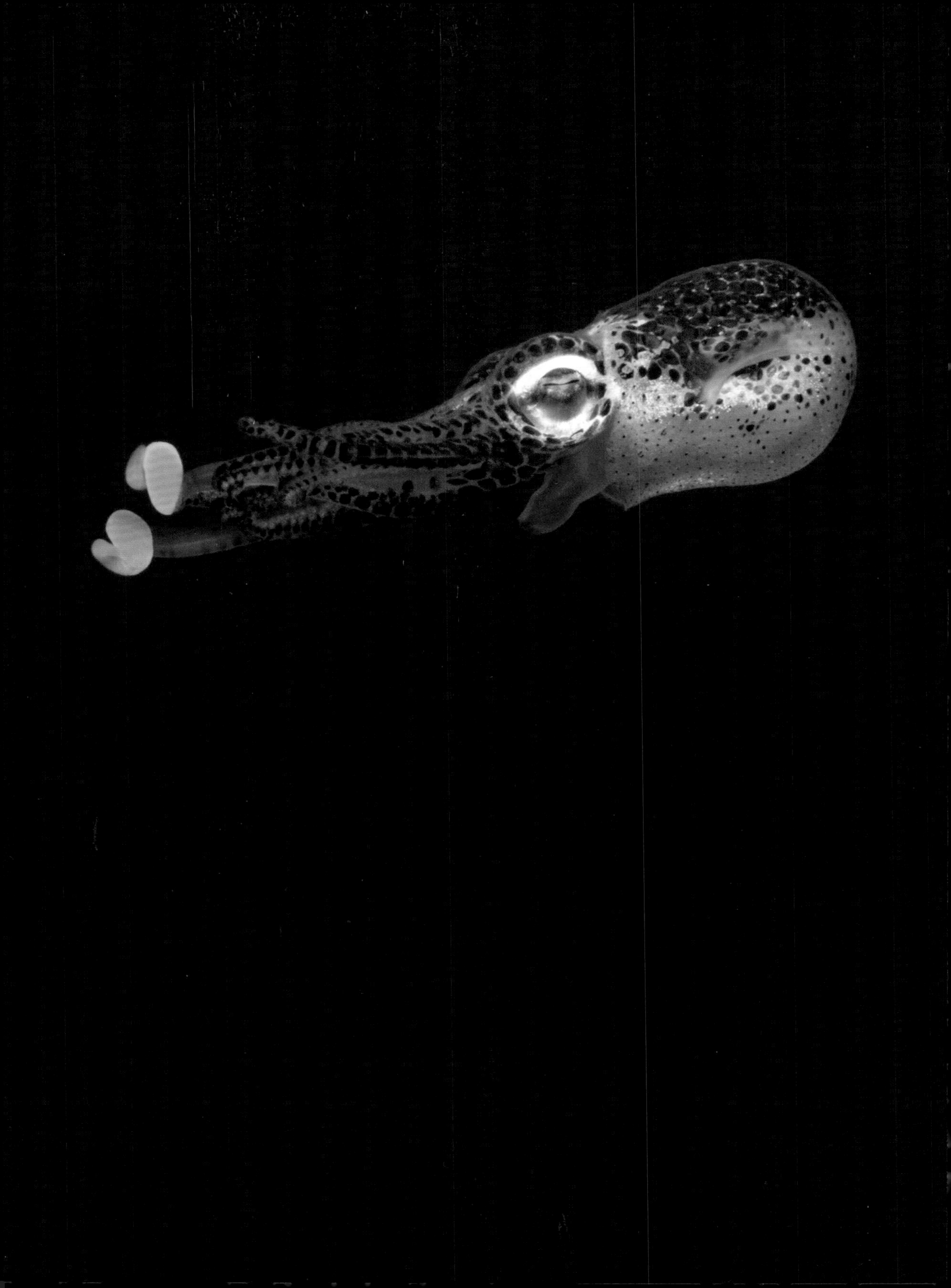

BIO*luminescence*

Nature *and* Science *at* Work

MARC ZIMMER

TWENTY-FIRST CENTURY BOOKS / MINNEAPOLIS

TO MY PARENTS AND ALL THE READERS OF THIS BOOK, MAY YOU ALWAYS APPRECIATE NATURE'S LIGHTS.

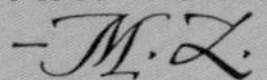

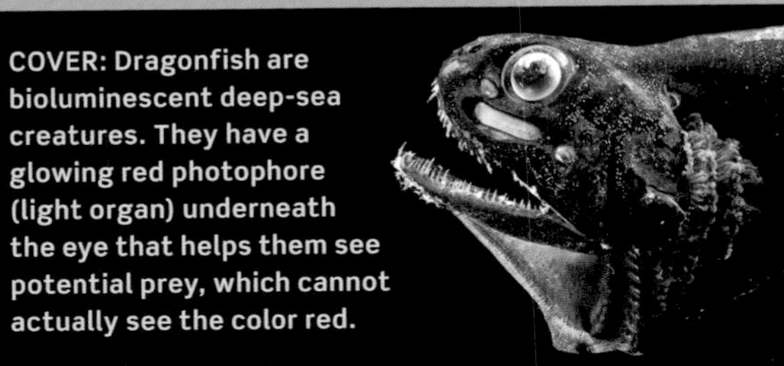

COVER: Dragonfish are bioluminescent deep-sea creatures. They have a glowing red photophore (light organ) underneath the eye that helps them see potential prey, which cannot actually see the color red.

Twenty-First Century Books
A division of Lerner Publishing Group, Inc.
241 First Avenue North
Minneapolis, MN 55401 USA

Main body text set in Chaparral Pro 11/14
Typeface provided by Adobe Systems.

For reading levels and more information, look up this title at www.lernerbooks.com.

Library of Congress Cataloging-in-Publication Data

Zimmer, Marc, author.
Bioluminescence : nature and science at work / by Marc Zimmer.
pages cm
Includes bibliographical references and index.
ISBN 978-1-4677-5784-3 (lib. bdg. : alk. paper) — ISBN 978-1-4677-8800-7 (ebook PDF)
1. Bioluminescence. 2. Green fluorescent protein. I. Title.
QH641.Z56 2016
572'.4358—dc23 2014025675

Manufactured in the United States of America
1 – PC – 7/15/15

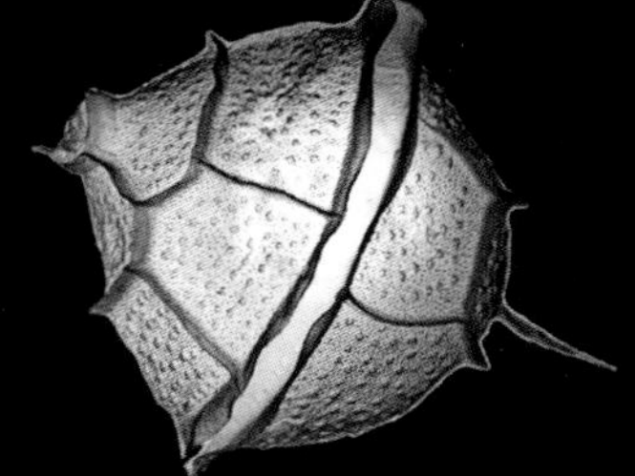

Contents

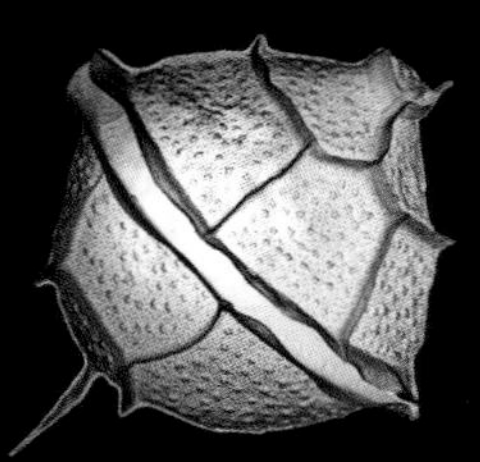

CHAPTER 1

GIVING OFF *Light*

The bioluminescent glow of fireflies is easily visible at night. Firefly bioluminescence is almost 100 percent efficient, losing very little energy in the form of heat during light production.

When the first fireflies come out in summer, it's hard not to smile. After the long winter months, these flying lightbulbs are a sight to see. Why do they flash their lights? Can their lights cause them to overheat? And why do they emit light in the first place?

Fireflies and other living organisms that give off light are called bioluminescent organisms. The word *bioluminescence* comes from the Greek word *bios* (living) and the Latin word *lumen* (light). Through the process of evolution, many species have developed the ability to bioluminesce, or to make and emit their own light. Different species use different chemistries to bioluminesce, and they produce their light for a variety of reasons, including communication, hunting, and self-defense. Bioluminescence is a unique and fascinating adaptation found in most of the animal kingdom. It is so common that half of all known phyla (groupings of animals that all have the same body type) contain some bioluminescent species.

Discovering Lucifer

In the nineteenth century, French physiologist Raphaël Dubois discovered that bioluminescence requires at least two different chemicals. In 1885 he ground up the abdomens of some bioluminescent Brazilian headlight beetles (also known as South American fireflies) and found that by adding cold water to the beetle mush, he could make a glowing solution. With time the glow of the brightly shining solution became fainter.

If Dubois added hot water to a fresh solution of beetle mush, it did not glow. However, if he waited for the hot solution to cool and then added some of it to the solution that was no longer glowing, it would start to glow again.

Dubois hypothesized that both solutions contained two important components. In the cold solution, both components gave off light until one of the two ran out. In the hot solution, the heat destroyed one of the components and no light was produced. When Dubois added the cooled solution to the spent cold solution, that solution started to glow again. This was because the component that had survived the heat was the one that had been used up in the cold solution. Dubois named the molecule that was consumed in the light-producing cold-water reaction luciferin. He called the component that was destroyed in the hot water luciferase. Both terms come from the name Lucifer, the Bible's fallen angel of light.

Dubois then repeated the experiment with some bioluminescent clams and got the same results. At the time, scientists knew that enzymes are temperature sensitive and that their function is to make chemical reactions occur faster and more efficiently. For this reason, Dubois proposed that luciferase—the temperature-sensitive component—was an enzyme. He was correct, and in the twenty-first century, scientists know that nearly every bioluminescent organism has a luciferin molecule and a luciferase enzyme, which react and produce light. Every bioluminescent species has a different kind of luciferase, but only seven types of luciferins exist. Scientists refer to them as firefly, snail, earthworm, bacteria, dinoflagellate, coelenterazine (squid and jellyfish), and *Cypridina* (seed shrimp) luciferins.

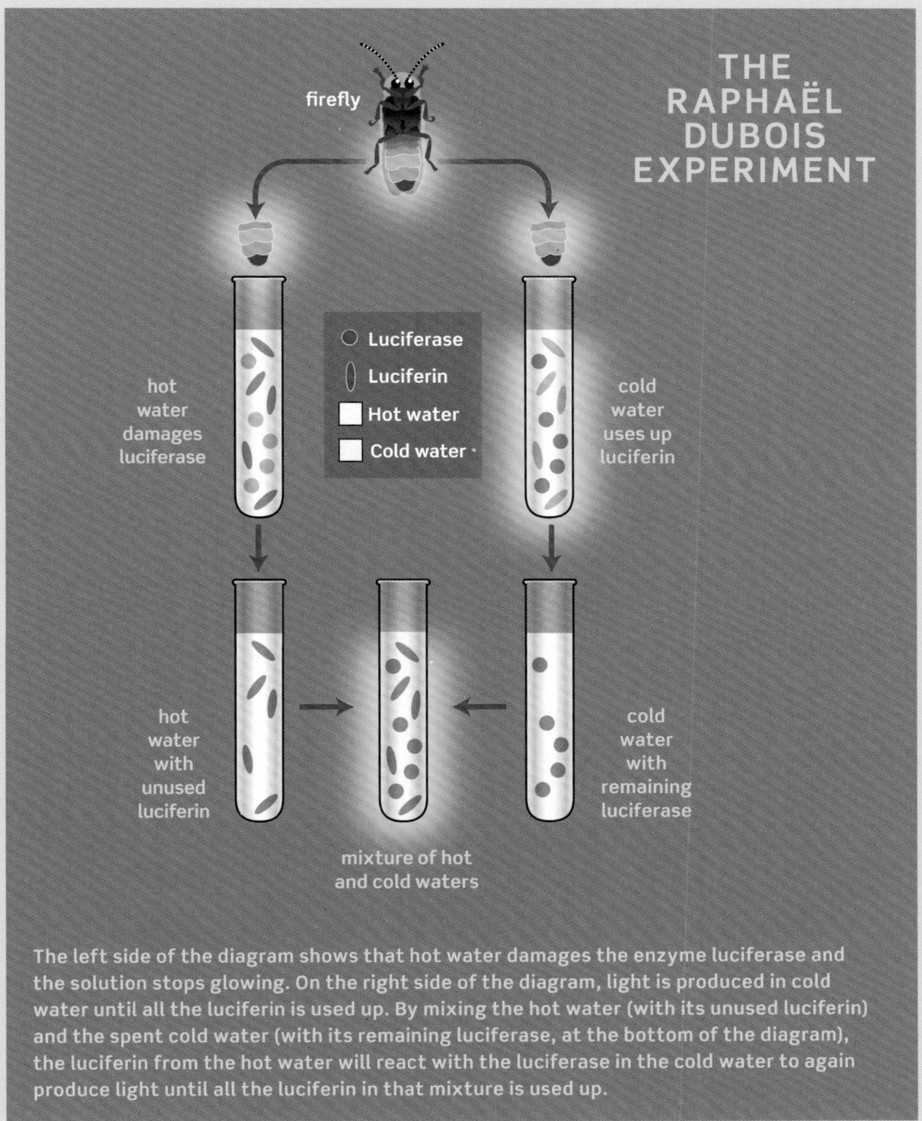

The left side of the diagram shows that hot water damages the enzyme luciferase and the solution stops glowing. On the right side of the diagram, light is produced in cold water until all the luciferin is used up. By mixing the hot water (with its unused luciferin) and the spent cold water (with its remaining luciferase, at the bottom of the diagram), the luciferin from the hot water will react with the luciferase in the cold water to again produce light until all the luciferin in that mixture is used up.

A Nobel Glow

The eerie glow of bioluminescent organisms has intrigued humans for centuries. And although scientists don't understand all facets of nature's lights, they have harnessed their glow and can use them in a myriad of ways.

THE COLOR SPECTRUM

Light is a form of electromagnetic radiation that sometimes behaves like a wave and sometimes like a particle. The distance between successive waves of light is called the wavelength. The shorter the wavelength, the higher the energy of the radiation. Scientists refer to the range of wavelengths—from short, high-intensity waves to long, low intensity waves—as the electromagnetic spectrum. Human eyes can see only a very small fraction of the electromagnetic spectrum, which scientists call the visible spectrum.

The colors in the visible spectrum range from red, which has the longest wavelength and the least energy, to orange, yellow, green, blue, and violet, which has the shortest, most energetic wavelengths. Most deep-sea fish have more limited vision than humans and can see only blue light. However, some creatures, such as the mantis shrimp, can see ultraviolet, visible, and infrared radiation. Ultraviolet radiation has more energy than visible light, while infrared light has less energy than red light.

The sun emits the entire range of the electromagnetic spectrum. Most of the dangerous, high-energy radiation is absorbed in the outer atmosphere before it reaches Earth. Sunlight is Earth's most important energy source, and most of this energy is in the form of visible light, particularly yellow light.

VISIBLE LIGHT SPECTRUM

low energy/
long wavelengths

high energy/
short wavelengths

Light wavelengths are measured in nanometers and radiate energy that is measured as electron volts. Visible light that humans can see *(PICTURED IN THE CHART ABOVE)* range from high-energy violet and blue on one end of the spectrum to lower-energy orange and red on the other. Many animals, including some bioluminescent creatures, can see well beyond what is visible to the human eye.

One of the most important applications involves using bioluminescence as a microscope to improve science and medicine in new and colorful ways. For example, laboratory scientists can genetically modify malaria parasites (*Plasmodium falciparum*) with bioluminescent proteins and track the resulting glow as the parasites leave the mosquito's proboscis (mouthpart) to bite a mouse. Scientists can then track the parasites as they escape from the mouse's white blood cells and make their way to hide in the liver of their new host.

Bioluminescent proteins are so useful to twenty-first-century medicine that two groups of scientists were awarded the Nobel Prize in Chemistry for their work with these proteins. Osamu Shimomura, Martin Chalfie, and Roger Tsien received the Nobel Prize in Chemistry in 2008 for their discovery and development of the green fluorescent protein, or GFP. Eric Betzig, Stefan Hell, and William Moerner were awarded the prize in 2014 for their work with super-resolution microscopy, or techniques based on fluorescent proteins that allow microscopes to image objects smaller than half the wavelength of light.

CHAPTER 2
NATURE'S *Lights*

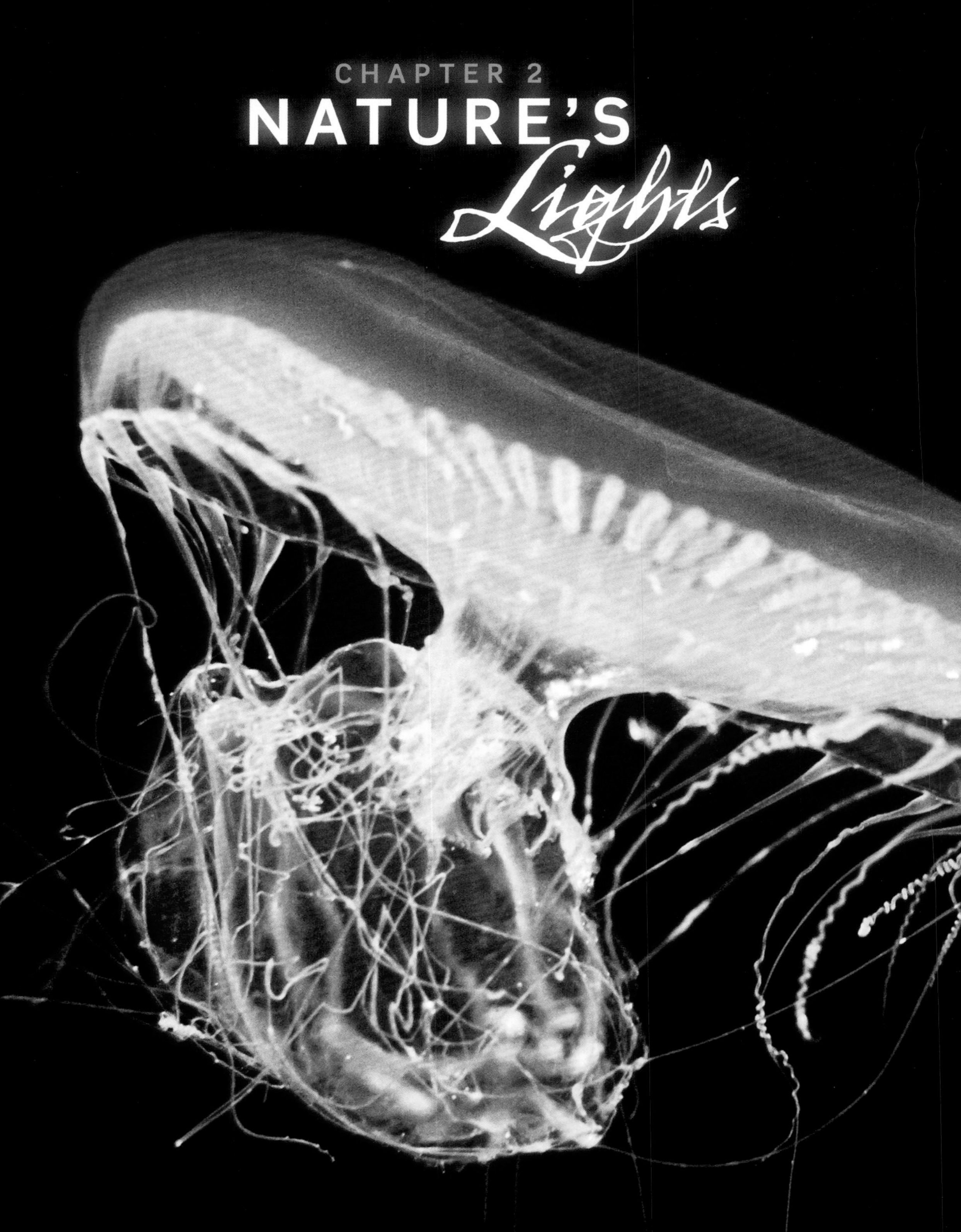

Over hundreds of millions of years, animals have evolved to give off light to defend themselves, to communicate, to attract food, and to find mating partners. Most bioluminescent species—such as luminescent squid and octopuses, glowing jellyfish and shrimp, as well as luminous fish and bacteria—live in the world's oceans. The average depth of the ocean floor is 2.4 miles (3.9 kilometers). Natural light cannot penetrate this far, so most areas of the oceans are completely dark. Scientists estimate that 80 to 90 percent of all deep-sea invertebrates and vertebrates living in these dark depths are bioluminescent. In fact, scientists have determined that every cubic meter of seawater has at least one bioluminescent organism. These creatures are the only source of natural light in the ocean.

Sea creatures have no place to hide in the open ocean. As a result, most marine organisms move to these deeper, darker waters to evade predators. Most fishes and crustaceans living in the pitch-black depths of the ocean have eyes. Scientists have determined that the only use for these eyes is to see the bioluminescence of other organisms, which is an indicator of the supreme importance of bioluminescence to organisms that live in the oceans.

In freshwater, ambient light helps aquatic creatures see, so they don't need bioluminescence to find prey or to communicate. They also don't need it for defense because rocks, grasses, and mud offer numerous places for them to hide from predators. For this reason, freshwater organisms don't have to give off light, and only a handful of them—such as some species of limpets—bioluminesce. The same is true on land, so terrestrial bioluminescence is not very common. Only fireflies, fungi, centipedes, millipedes, snails, fungus gnats, and earthworms have evolved to give off light in their dark, land-based habitats.

Crystal jellyfish *(Aequorea victoria)* are a bioluminescent jellyfish, although not all jellyfish are bioluminescent. *A. victoria* lives in the Pacific Ocean off the coast of western North America.

THE FIVE OCEAN ZONES

Oceanographers, the scientists who study the ocean, divide the ocean into five different zones. Bioluminescent creatures mostly live in the middle and the lower zones. The intensity and the color spectrum (ranging from less visible reds to more visible blues) of the sunlight penetrating the water changes with depth. The farther down in the water, the darker the environment. For example, at the top of the ocean's mesopelagic zone, 656 feet (200 meters) from the surface, the intensity of the light is one hundredth of what it is at the epipelagic zone, just below the surface of the water. At the bottom of the mesopelagic zone, at 3,281 feet (1,000 m), the light drops to one trillionth of its initial intensity.

In the mesopelagic zone and the zones below it, all the colors of the sun's light spectrum except blue have been absorbed by the water. Blue light travels the farthest in water. For this reason, most bioluminescent marine creatures give off blue light and can see blue light better than any other color. No sunlight penetrates the bathypelagic, abyssopelagic, and hadalpelagic zones, where more than 80 percent of the organisms are bioluminescent.

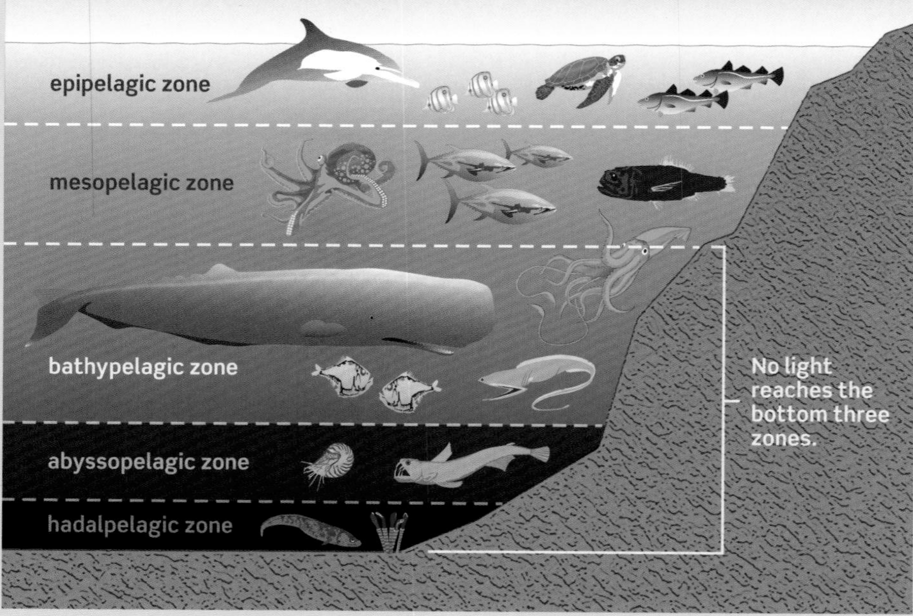

A deep sea shrimp *(Acanthephyra purpurea)* spits out bioluminescent slime to defend itself against a much bigger predator, the viper fish *(Chauliodus danae)*.

Bioluminescence as Defense

Defense against predators is the most common use of bioluminescence, particularly in deep-water marine environments, where most bioluminescent species live. When threatened, some species of deep-sea shrimp, for example, will vomit brightly luminescent blue-green slime directly at their enemies. This not only frightens the predator but also makes it difficult for the predator to see and track the shrimp.

The most abundant vertebrate in the world, in terms of sheer numbers, is the bristlemouth. A small fish with bristle-like teeth, the bristlemouth grows no longer than 3 inches (8 centimeters) and is found between 500 and 1,500 feet (152 and 457 m) under the ocean surface. The bristlemouth, which ranges in color from black to silver, has two rows of photophores (light-emitting organs) on the underside of its head and stomach. The colors of the bristlemouth's bioluminescence—green or red—blend in with those of the lighter-colored waters above. For this reason, when predators from below look up toward the bristlemouth, they

The Hawaiian bobtail squid spends most of its day buried in the sand of shallow coastal waters of the western Pacific Ocean. At night it swims around looking for food. The colors created by the squid's bioluminescent bacteria, which live in the squid's light organs, blend in with the colors of lighter waters above the squid. This form of camouflage is called counter-illumination.

do not see the fish's silhouette at all. This defensive use of luminescence as camouflage is quite common among deep-sea creatures and is known as counter-illumination

The Hawaiian bobtail squid is a champion counter-illuminator. A native of Pacific coastal waters near Hawaii, the squid relies on bacteriogenic bioluminescence to camouflage its body in marine waters. In this form of bioluminescence, an animal lives in a symbiotic (mutually dependent) relationship with bioluminescent bacteria in its body. The squid's bioluminescent bacteria live in light organs in the squid's mantle (the body parts behind the head). As with the bristlemouth, an illuminated bobtail squid is invisible to hungry predators swimming beneath.

The glowing bacteria and the squid have an excellent symbiotic relationship that benefits them both. The bacteria get a safe, warm breeding location inside the squid. In turn, the bacteria light up the squid's periphery and hide the animal from its enemies. The squid and the bacteria can both live independently, but they do much better together. Scientists don't know exactly how, but the squid lets only bioluminescent bacteria live in its photophores. The squid will even eject bioluminescent bacteria when they don't produce enough light.

When baby squid first hatch, they have no bioluminescent bacteria at all. In just a few hours, however, bacteria find their way to the baby squid light organs and rapidly multiply in their new homes. With billions of bacteria in place, the light organs then develop the mechanical features that allow for bioluminescence. These include a lens, light detectors, a reflector, and a shutter. The bacteria give off a steady intensity of light. But the squid uses the light detectors on top of its head and the shutter to regulate the amount of light it gives off. With these tools, the squid can match the intensity of light it is emitting to the amount of sunlight that is penetrating the depths of the ocean in which it is swimming. In this way, the squid can regulate its own counter-illumination.

After they have settled in the squid's light organs, the bacteria themselves also change, losing their tails and becoming smaller. The light organ of a single adult Hawaiian bobtail squid can accommodate up to one trillion bioluminescent bacteria. Each photophore has so many bacteria and they multiply so rapidly that every morning the photophore evicts most of its glowing residents to prevent overpopulation and to keep a healthy, vibrant environment of bioluminescent bacteria in the light organs. Many of the evicted bacteria are then attracted to the light organs of young squid that are looking for bioluminescent bacteria of their own.

Dinoflagellates

Microorganisms known as dinoflagellates are very common in the ocean. In the Caribbean waters of Vieques, Puerto Rico, for example, 1 gallon (3.8 liters) of water can contain as many as 720,000 dinoflagellates. The microorganisms have two whirling tails. (*Dino* is the Greek word for "whirling," and *flagellae* is the Latin word for "whips," or tails.) When agitated at night—by waves, boats, or marine animals—some species

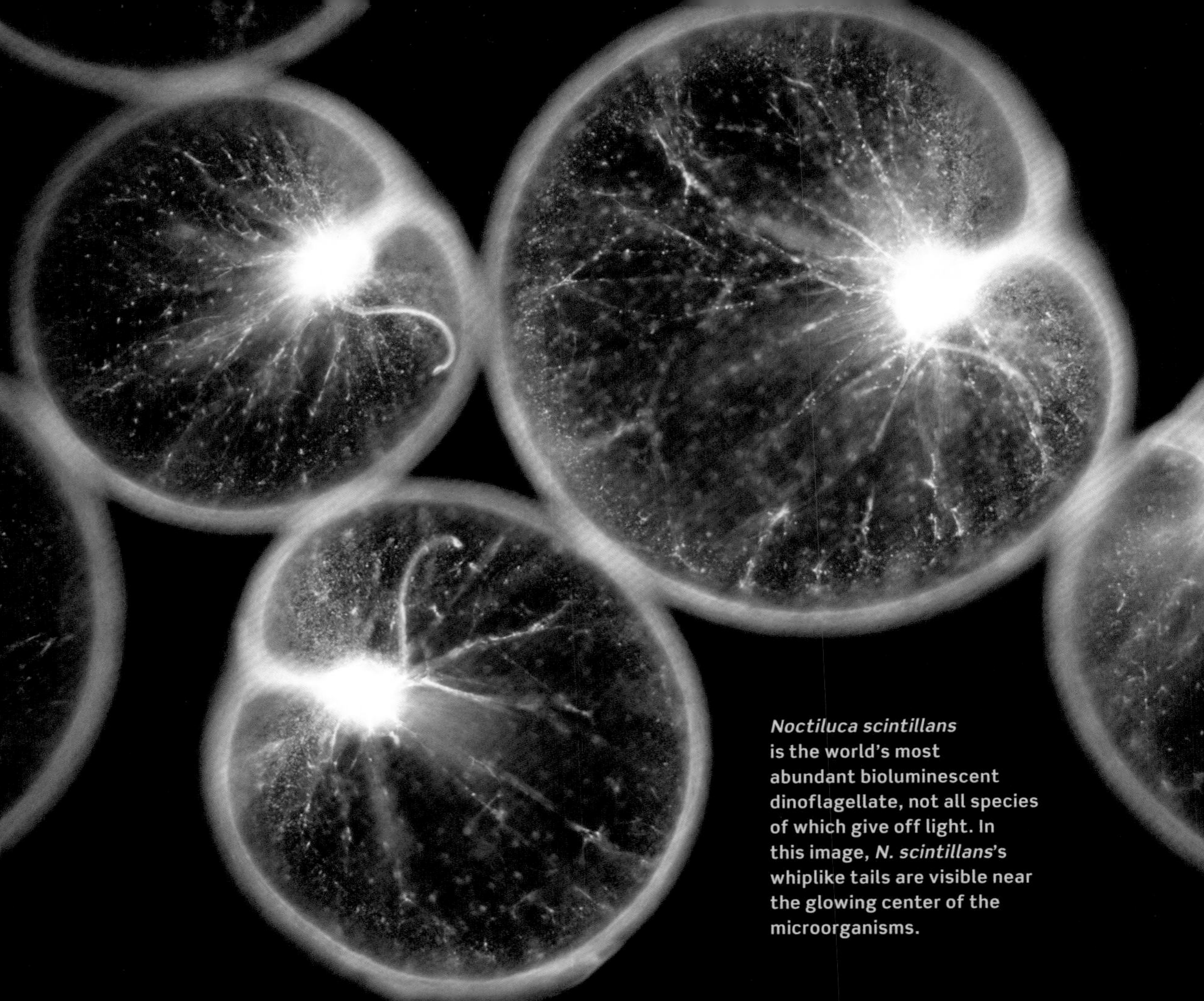

Noctiluca scintillans **is the world's most abundant bioluminescent dinoflagellate, not all species of which give off light. In this image, *N. scintillans*'s whiplike tails are visible near the glowing center of the microorganisms.**

of these microorganisms flash a greenish-blue light. They are autogenic (produced by the creature itself) bioluminescent organisms that use a luciferin/luciferase reaction to make light. At night, the bioluminescent reaction can be initiated if something touches either tail. Even at low concentrations, this sparkling light is visible on the surface of the water and is famous among visiting tourists. Not all dinoflagellates bioluminesce, however. Scientists think that the tiny, sightless dinoflagellates that do bioluminesce have developed the capability as a defense mechanism to dazzle their enemies. The light functions as a burglar alarm to chase away any fish that swim into a bloom of dinoflagellates.

Benjamin Franklin Enters the Picture

Throughout history the glow of dinoflagellates has led to much confusion and many misconceptions. In 1747, for example, American scholar-inventor Benjamin Franklin wrote about bioluminescent ocean waters, of which he had only read. He said that one could consider "the sea as the grand source of lightning, imagining its luminous appearance to be owing to electric fire, produced by friction between particles of water and those of salt." Because of his excellent reputation, Franklin's view of what he thought was the electrical nature of the luminescence sometimes observed in the oceans was well regarded. However, his conjecture was purely based on theory. Franklin lived in Philadelphia, far from an ocean, and had no opportunity to do experiments with seawater. Yet Franklin was an excellent scientist who was willing to change his mind if evidence did not support an idea.

By 1753, based on a letter from James Bowdoin, governor of Massachusetts and an amateur scientist, Franklin had changed his opinion on the origin of luminous seawater. In his 1769 book *Experiments and Observations on Electricity Made at Philadelphia in America, to Which Are Added Letters and Papers on Philosophical Subjects*, Franklin published the Bowdoin letter. In it, the governor reported that filtering what he referred to incorrectly as phosphorescent seawater through a cloth resulted in the removal of the light from the water. (Phosphorescence is the gradual release of light by an object caused by the absorption of light energy and not by an internal chemical reaction.) He wrote that the "said appearance might be caused by a great number of little animals, floating on the surface of the sea, which on being disturbed, might, by expanding their fins, or otherwise moving themselves, expose such a part of their bodies as exhibits a luminous appearance, somewhat in the manner of a glow-worm, or firefly." This letter was proof enough for Franklin to withdraw his support for the electrical theory and to fully support the bioluminescent organism theory, which twenty-first-century scientists know is indeed the correct explanation.

Bioluminescence through Time

The first reports of bioluminescence are not in Franklin's or Bowdoin's writings but in ancient Chinese and Indian literature. Early literature of the Middle East and the Indian subcontinent has numerous references to

GLOWING IN THE DARK

Bioluminescence and phosphorescence are two very different light-producing processes. When a chemical reaction in a living organism produces light, scientists call it bioluminescence. Phosphorescence, on the other hand, occurs when a molecule (which doesn't have to be in a living being) absorbs light energy of one wavelength and later returns it to the surroundings at a different, lower-energy wavelength. Glow-in-the-dark ceiling stars are good examples of phosphorescent objects. When a molecule absorbs light, scientists say the molecule is excited. Molecules absorb energy from (are excited by) sunlight and glowing lightbulbs in a room. Then they return that energy to the surroundings as visible light when it is dark.

Dinoflagellate light is produced through a chemical reaction in the microorganism itself. The organism doesn't phosphoresce, it bioluminesces. So the marine luminescence to which Governor James Bowdoin referred in the 1700s was not phosphorescence. It was bioluminescence.

the firefly, but writers were not very impressed by the amount of light the firefly produced. In fact, the early Arabic-language name for a firefly is derived from the word for a man who is so stingy that he makes a fire too small to be of any use.

In the 300s BCE, the ancient Greek philosopher and scientist Aristotle mentioned a quality of bioluminescence he called "cold light. By this he meant that the light produced by some jellyfish, fireflies, and fungi is not associated with an increase in heat, as are other forms of light. Scientists of the twenty-first century still refer to luminescence as cold light.

Pliny the Elder (23–79 CE), a famous ancient Roman naturalist, saw many parts of the world during his military career and observed many new and exotic species. His descriptions of light-producing organisms were among the most complete and accurate for his time. Before he died in the eruption of Italy's Mount Vesuvius—an eruption famous for destroying the city of Pompeii—he described the bioluminescence of snails, jellyfish, lantern fish, and fungi. He reported that glowworms "shine like fires at night time" and that luminous fungi could be used as medicines.

Pliny the Elder also wrote about an edible clam that squirted phosphorescent green slime when it was frightened. Anyone who ate the clams ended up with a pair of glowing green lips. The Romans got a kick out of this bizarre spectacle, and for a while, glow-in-the-dark banquets were a popular first-century eating craze. Pliny also reported that a paste made from the luminous materials of the clam and then mixed with flour, honey, and water would produce light, even up to a year later. In book 9 of Pliny's *Naturalis Historiae*, a scientific encyclopedia of natural history published in the 70s CE, he wrote that the clams "shine in the darkness with a bright light when other light is removed, and . . . glitter both in the mouth of persons [chewing] them and in their hands, and even on the floor and on their clothes when drops fall from them."

This Japanese woodblock print from around 1880 shows *hotaru-gari*, or firefly hunting. Fireflies were common pets and were kept in traditional firefly cages woven with straw.

Burning Angels

Fireflies especially have fascinated people in Japan. Since the 700s CE, the firefly has been a metaphor in Japanese poetry for passionate love and hearts on fire. In Japanese mythology, the firefly's eerie lights are also thought to symbolize the souls of the dead. Hundreds of haiku (a short form of stylized Japanese verse) have been written about what Japanese poets refer to as burning angels (a metaphor for fireflies commonly used to signify that they are the souls of the dead). Firefly viewing was most popular in Japan during the Edo period (1603–1867). In the twenty-first century, many Japanese people go to the countryside to watch fireflies, and the annual firefly festival outside of the Japanese city of Kyoto is very popular. The festival includes traditional music, dance, and a tea ceremony in which six hundred fireflies are released at the Shimogamo Shrine.

Bioluminescence as Communication for Mating

In nature, bioluminescence can also be used as a form of communication, particularly among land-based animals such as fireflies. Every species of firefly has a distinctive pattern of flashes to which only individuals of that same species respond.

The intensity of the light largely depends on the species of firefly. For example, about six thousand females from the common European firefly (*Lampyris noctiluca*) together produce light of the same brightness as one candle. Only thirty-seven to forty females of the South American firefly (*Pyrophorus noctilucus*) are required to attain that same intensity.

Adult fireflies live no longer than two weeks, and they spend all their time and energy finding a mate. When looking for a partner, male fireflies zip around, flashing their light. This occurs mainly at dusk and early night, when the light is easily seen. The specific flashing sequence unique to each firefly species is an important evolutionary mechanism that prevents fireflies of different species from interbreeding and thereby producing infertile offspring.

Sitting on the ground, a female will recognize the sequence of flashes of males belonging to her species. The sequence is a sort of password that is characteristic only of that particular firefly species. In the firefly world, brighter is better. In fact, researchers using artificial pulses of light have shown that female fireflies respond best to males with the species-correct flashing sequence and the brightest flashes. If the females are interested, they emit a sequence of species-specific flashes informing the male that they would like to meet. In many firefly species, the males have large, protruding eyes to readily detect even the faintest female response.

Female anglerfish have a bioluminescent dorsal fin at the front of their mouth. The light at the tip of the fin is created by millions of glowing bacteria and lures unsuspecting prey toward the fish. Scientists refer to this type of bioluminescence—created by symbiotic bacteria—as bacteriogenic luminescence.

Bioluminescence for Finding Food

Just as moths are attracted to bright lights in the dark of night, so too are small fishes, shrimp, and other sea creatures in the gloomy depths of the ocean. So some inhabitants of the deep ocean use their lights to lure their dinner to them.

More than two hundred different species of deep-sea anglerfish live in the ocean, all below 2,952 feet (900 m). They have evolved a unique bacteriogenic method of catching their meals. The female anglerfish has a long, thin dorsal fin that protrudes in front of her mouth. At the tip of the

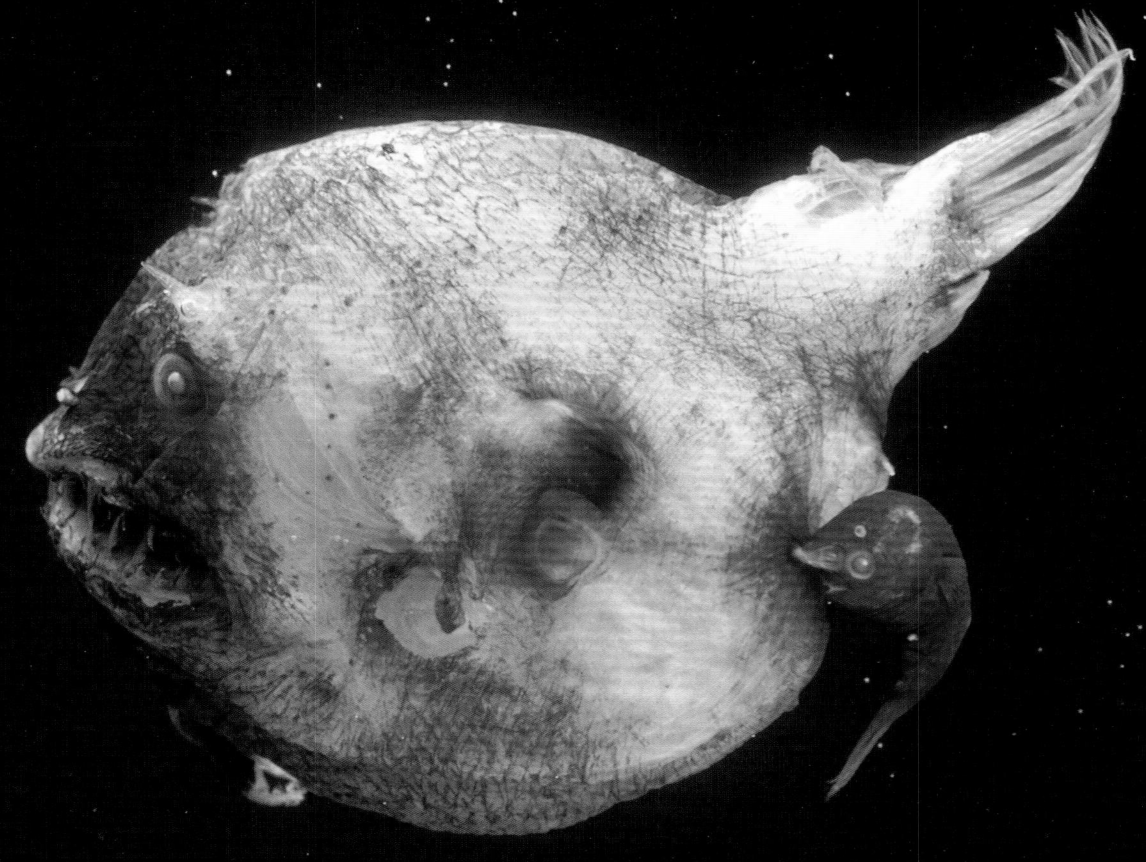

After mating, some types of male anglerfish live in a parasitic relationship with the female. Parasitic males *(FAR RIGHT)* are typically much smaller than females and have poorly developed jaws and digestive tracts. So the parasitic male relies on the female host for food for the rest of his life.

fin are millions of light-producing bacteria, which live in symbiosis with the anglerfish.

In the dark depths of the anglerfish's world, the light emitted by the gently oscillating anglerfish lightbulb looks like a small and inviting meal. Deep-sea predators are attracted to the lure. Little do they realize the danger of the small flash of light. Underneath it, lurking in the dark, is the large anglerfish mouth, just waiting to make a meal of the unsuspecting predator.

Male anglerfish grow to a mere 2.5 inches (6.4 cm) in length, while the females can reach a whopping 47 inches (119 cm). Male anglerfish have no dorsal fin for luring prey, however. Instead, before mating, they rely on sight to hunt for food. After mating, the male anglerfish attaches himself to the female in what becomes a parasitic relationship. The male attaches for the rest of his life, connecting to the female's bloodstream. In exchange for his sperm, the female provides protection and food. Because the female lures all the food, the male no longer needs his eyes and slowly loses his sight. The female, on the other hand, gets a lifelong mating partner. Some females have as many as six males attached to their bodies!

SEEING RED

Some species of dragonfish, which live in deep waters of the Atlantic Ocean, have evolved a very tricky way to find their prey. Because red light doesn't travel very far in water, most deep-sea organisms don't need to see red, so their eyes do not perceive this color. To take advantage of this, dragonfish have small, red bioluminescent photophores just under their eyes. Prey and predators alike cannot see the red spotlights in action, so the dragonfish can pounce without warning on its prey and quickly identify predators to escape from them safely.

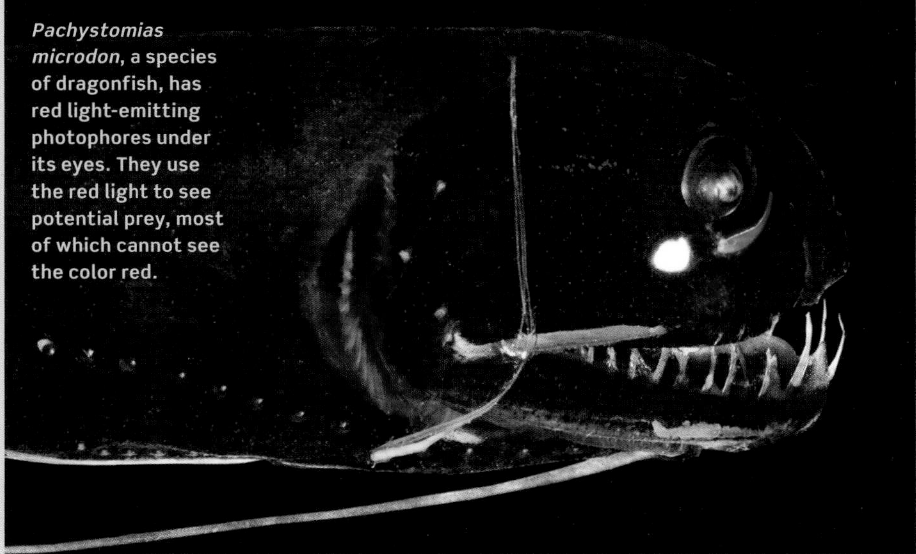

Pachystomias microdon, a species of dragonfish, has red light-emitting photophores under its eyes. They use the red light to see potential prey, most of which cannot see the color red.

CHAPTER 3

MODEL ORGANISM: *Fireflies*

Most fireflies are nocturnal, spending the day in grasses, bushes, and trees. Not all firefly species glow, however. Of those that do, each species has a recognizable pattern of flashes and unique intensity of light.

Scientists regularly study certain types of common, nonhuman, living species to learn more about the biology of other living organisms. These frequently studied species exist—and can be reproduced in a lab—in large numbers and are called model organisms. Mice, fruit flies, bacteria (*Escherichia coli*), and roundworms (*Caernorhabditis elegans*) are common model organisms.

In the world of bioluminescence, fireflies are a model organism because they are among the most frequently observed bioluminescent organisms and are found in large numbers on every continent except Antarctica. For this reason, they are the most commonly studied bioluminescent organism and are the source of much of the knowledge of light production in living organisms.

In different parts of the world, fireflies are also known as lightning bugs, glow flies, glowworms, fire devils, and blinkies. Of the approximate 2,000 species of fireflies in the world, more than 170 species are found in the United States, most of them east of Kansas. In fact, in 1974 the eastern state of Pennsylvania adopted *Photuris pennsylvanica*, a firefly, as its official state insect.

Like other beetles, fireflies *(RIGHT)* have hard wing covers and toothlike mandibles.

Fireflies are insects, but they do not belong to the fly family. They are actually beetles. The main characteristic that distinguishes beetles from all other insects is that they have hard wing covers, while insect wings consist of a thin membrane supported by a system of veins. The name *beetle* comes from the Old English word *bitan*, which means "to bite" and refers to the ability of beetles to chew and gnaw their hard food sources with their toothlike mandibles. In contrast, true flies have spongy mouthparts, which they use to suck the blood they feed on. Because fireflies have hard wing covers and mandibles, they are beetles.

Most firefly species are nocturnal and spend the daylight hours in the shade of grasses, bushes, and trees. All juvenile fireflies glow, but the adults of some species cannot glow. Every species of glowing firefly has a distinctive pattern of flashes. The intensity of the light produced depends on the species.

Danger: Bioluminescence!

Flying through the dark night flashing a light may attract female fireflies, but it is not a good way for male fireflies to hide from predators. Fireflies have many natural enemies, such as birds, frogs, lizards, and spiders, that have no problem finding their flashing prey. Yet not all male fireflies are vulnerable. The males of some species of fireflies release a poisonous chemical when threatened by an enemy. Scientists have found the chemical structure of this material to be similar to that in the venoms of Chinese toads. Even though it does not glow, this venom is called lucibufagin, a combination of the Latin words *lux* (meaning "light") and *bufo* (meaning "toad"). When the male firefly is challenged by a predator, the firefly automatically releases a protective fluid that contains enough of the repellent lucibufagin to drive off the hunter and avoid being eaten.

Females of some species of fireflies do not have lucibufagin, making them more susceptible to hungry predators. However, females of some types of firefly, such as the North American *Photuris*, have found a rather nasty way to get over their vulnerability. Once they have found a mate of their own species and have successfully mated, they wait for a male from a different species to come looking for a mate. When the male sends out his interrogatory flash sequence, the female is able to mimic the correct species-specific response for females from any one of eleven different firefly species.

The ill-fated male is unable to resist the false mating call and comes to the female to try his luck in the antenna dance. In this interaction, the two fireflies touch each other's antenna to confirm that their potential partner has the correct smell. Before the male firefly realizes that the female doesn't smell right—that she has tricked him into thinking she is

During courtship *(RIGHT)*, male and female fireflies of the same species use their bioluminescent flash patterns to communicate with each other. As a defense mechanism, some females can mimic the flash sequence of males outside the species, lure the males to them, and eat them.

one of his species—she devours him. However, the female does not eat the male because she is hungry. Instead, by eating the male, the female *Photuris* takes in the male's lucibufagin and is no longer vulnerable to enemies. The females also pass the foul-tasting lucibufagin to their eggs and offspring, thereby protecting them as well.

Citizen Science

Since Raphaël Dubois's nineteenth-century work with luciferin and luciferase, scientists have known that at least these two compounds are required to produce the firefly's flashes of light. But by the 1940s, William McElroy, a professor of biochemistry at Johns Hopkins University in Baltimore, Maryland, knew that there had to be more to it than that.

To find out what was happening inside the fireflies, McElroy needed lots of fireflies, many more than he and his students could possibly hope to catch themselves. McElroy decided to recruit local schoolchildren to do his firefly hunting for him. In 1947 he offered local kids twenty-five cents for every one hundred fireflies they brought to his labs, as well as a ten-dollar prize for the person who handed in the most fireflies. In the first year,

Professor William McElroy collected thousands of fireflies in the 1940s—with the help of kids—to research bioluminescence. He discovered that the chemical adenosine triphosphate is the energy source for the bioluminescent glow produced by fireflies.

ATP

Adenosine triphosphate, or ATP, is an amazing molecule. Every cell in the human body has about one billion ATP molecules. ATP provides the energy necessary in all living cells for heat, nerve conduction, and muscle contraction. The molecule is responsible for making our hearts beat and our brains think. As a person needs energy throughout the day, the body breaks down ATP molecules, uses them up, and replaces them with new ATP molecules in a matter of minutes. In fact, in a typical day, a person can produce and use up half the body's weight in ATP.

Biochemist William McElroy wondered whether ATP could be the energy source for the light produced by fireflies. It turned out that it was. Through experimentation McElroy found that when he added ATP to mixtures of luciferin and luciferase from firefly abdomens, the mixtures started glowing. The more ATP he added, the brighter the firefly extract glowed.

McElroy netted forty thousand fireflies. Ten-year-old Morgan Bucher Jr. won the ten-dollar prize. McElroy's army of firefly catchers steadily grew in size, and by the 1960s, he was collecting between five hundred thousand and one million fireflies each year.

McElroy knew that the light-producing reactions in fireflies occur in cells called photocytes, which are in the insects' abdomens. Laboratory assistants and graduate students dried thousands of fireflies and then separated their abdomens from their heads. By studying the abdominal photocytes, McElroy figured out that in fireflies four chemicals must come together in the photocytes to produce light. These chemicals are oxygen, adenosine triphosphate (ATP), luciferin, and luciferase. (Not all bioluminescent creatures require ATP to glow, however.) In the firefly, the chemical combination is a very controlled process, and the light the insect gives off is released in a precise Morse code–like sequence.

Nearly everything McElroy learned from his fireflies is true for all bioluminescent beetles. His work was key to confirming that every known bioluminescent organism on Earth requires oxygen, a luciferin, and a luciferase to make light.

CHAPTER 4

PUTTING BIO*luminescence* TO WORK

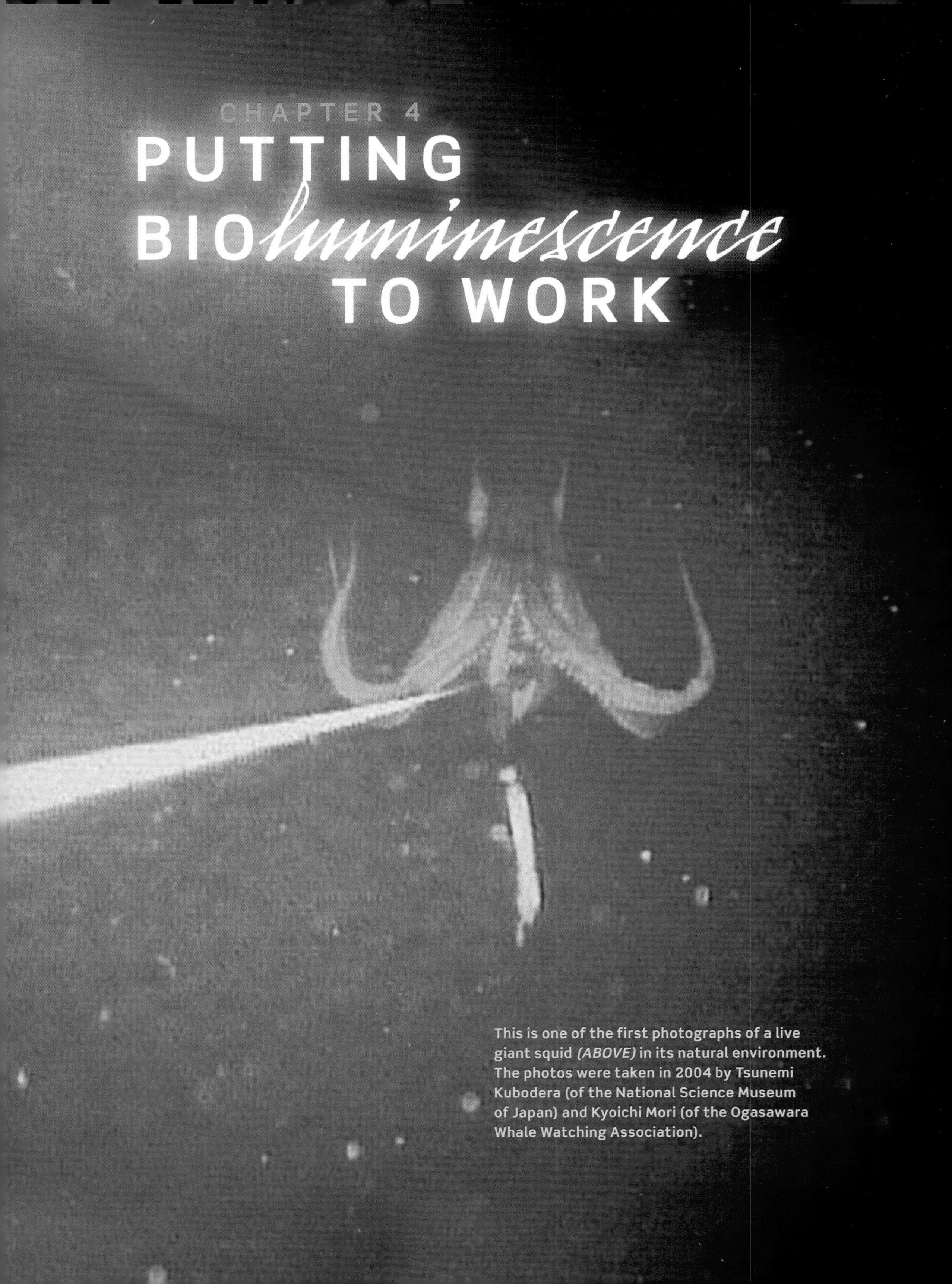

This is one of the first photographs of a live giant squid *(ABOVE)* in its natural environment. The photos were taken in 2004 by Tsunemi Kubodera (of the National Science Museum of Japan) and Kyoichi Mori (of the Ogasawara Whale Watching Association).

We know that giant squid with eyes as big as human heads exist because dead ones occasionally wash ashore, giving scientists the chance to dissect the 35-foot-long (11 m) wonders from the deep oceans. But before the twenty-first century, no one had actually filmed a live giant squid. That changed, thanks to Florida-based Edith (Edie) Widder, an oceanographer, marine biologist, and expert in bioluminescence. She put her knowledge of bioluminescence to work to learn more about giant squid.

Widder hypothesized that the bioluminescent rings of blue light that some jellyfish emit when they are attacked attract other, larger predators to drive off the initial attacker. To test her idea, she designed a bioluminescent jellyfish robot named Medusa, took it to sea, and recorded its ocean visitors. To Widder's delight, the pulsing blue lights of her robot lure attracted all kinds of creatures that had never before been seen.

In 2012 a Japanese giant squid expedition invited Widder and Medusa to join the team. They lowered the bioluminescent robot lure behind the expedition boat and into the

Edie Widder and her team were the first to film a live giant squid, in 2012. In the photo at right, she is entering the observation sphere of the Johnson-Sea-Link submersible. The submersible can dive to depths of 3,000 feet (914 m) carrying a pilot and scientist/observer in its observation sphere with two additional passengers in a separate rear dive chamber behind the sphere.

LUMINESCENCE IN THE ARTS

During the European Renaissance—an age of rich intellectual and artistic growth and achievement—artists such as Italian painter Caravaggio (1571-1610) used a powder of crushed fireflies to create paints with special light-sensitive qualities. In the twenty-first century, artists such as Chicago-based Hunter Cole are finding amazing ways to incorporate bioluminescence in their work. Cole paints with bioluminescent bacteria on agar plates (dishes with nutrients such as agar for growing microorganisms). She calls her works living drawings. As the bacteria grow on the plates over their two-week life cycle, the drawings change in appearance.

Even clothing designers find inspiration in bioluminescence. In a couture collection called Into the Deep, Chinese fashion designer Vega Wang created a collection of white clothing that featured blue electroluminescent patterns. (Electroluminescence is a glow of light created by an electric current running through a material.) The patterns were inspired by glowing jellyfish and other bioluminescent creatures.

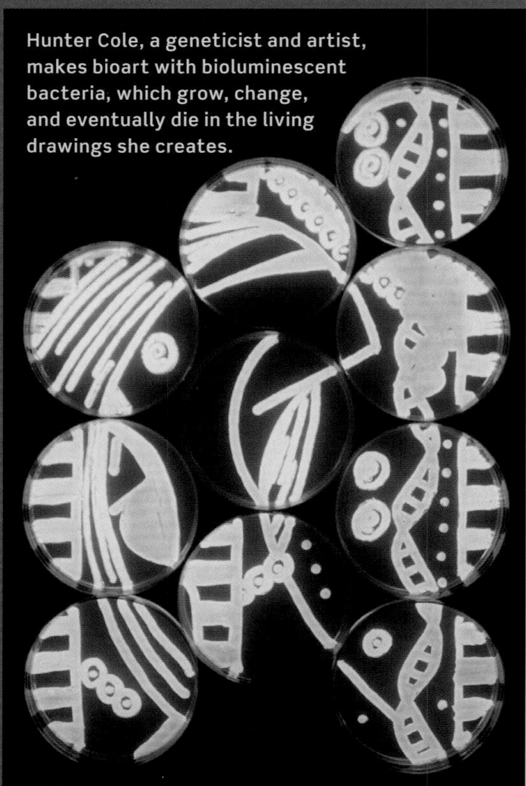

Hunter Cole, a geneticist and artist, makes bioart with bioluminescent bacteria, which grow, change, and eventually die in the living drawings she creates.

waters of the Pacific Ocean near Japan's Ogasawara Islands. A giant squid patrolling at 2,300 feet (701 m) could not resist the fake jellyfish. As the squid came to investigate Medusa, the expedition crew became the first to film a live giant squid.

Bioluminescent Test for Microbial Life

Like Widder's glowing Medusa, bioluminescence has many other applications in scientific research. For example, scientists know that ATP is a universal power source. If something is alive, it contains this molecule, and the addition of luciferin and luciferase to ATP will produce light in the presence of oxygen. Twenty-first-century scientists studying diseases typically require sterile conditions for their lab research. They rely on quick ATP bioluminescence tests to detect the presence of microbes (bacteria and other single-celled organisms) in their experiments. They know that a surface with no live bacteria will not glow when a mixture of luciferase and luciferin is applied. If bacteria are present, the ATP they contain will cause a bioluminescent glow. In the past, scientists had to rely on much slower processes to determine the presence of microbes. They would take a swab of the surface they were working on, add it to an agar plate (a dish with nutrients such as agar for growing microorganisms), and see if a microbial cell culture would grow. If it did, the researchers knew the surface was not sterile and microbes were living on the surface. They would then take additional precautions to ensure a germ-free environment for their work. The culture process can take days and is much less efficient than ATP testing.

Bioluminescence in the Search for Life on Mars

Is there life on Mars? The European Space Agency (ESA), the National Aeronautics and Space Administration (NASA), and the Russian Federal Space Agency have sent missions to the planet. One of their goals is to determine whether there are any forms of life on Mars. Through the early missions, scientists learned of the harsh conditions on the surface of the red planet. Mars is extremely cold and has very little, if any, oxygen or water, which are key to supporting life. For this reason, the astrobiologists of the time gave up all hope of ever finding life there. This changed during later Mars missions, when scientists obtained evidence that water had once flowed on Mars. They also discovered extremophiles on Earth.

Extremophiles are primitive organisms that flourish in extreme environments that lack oxygen. They are found in hydrothermal vents, which are fissures in the planet's surface that release geothermally

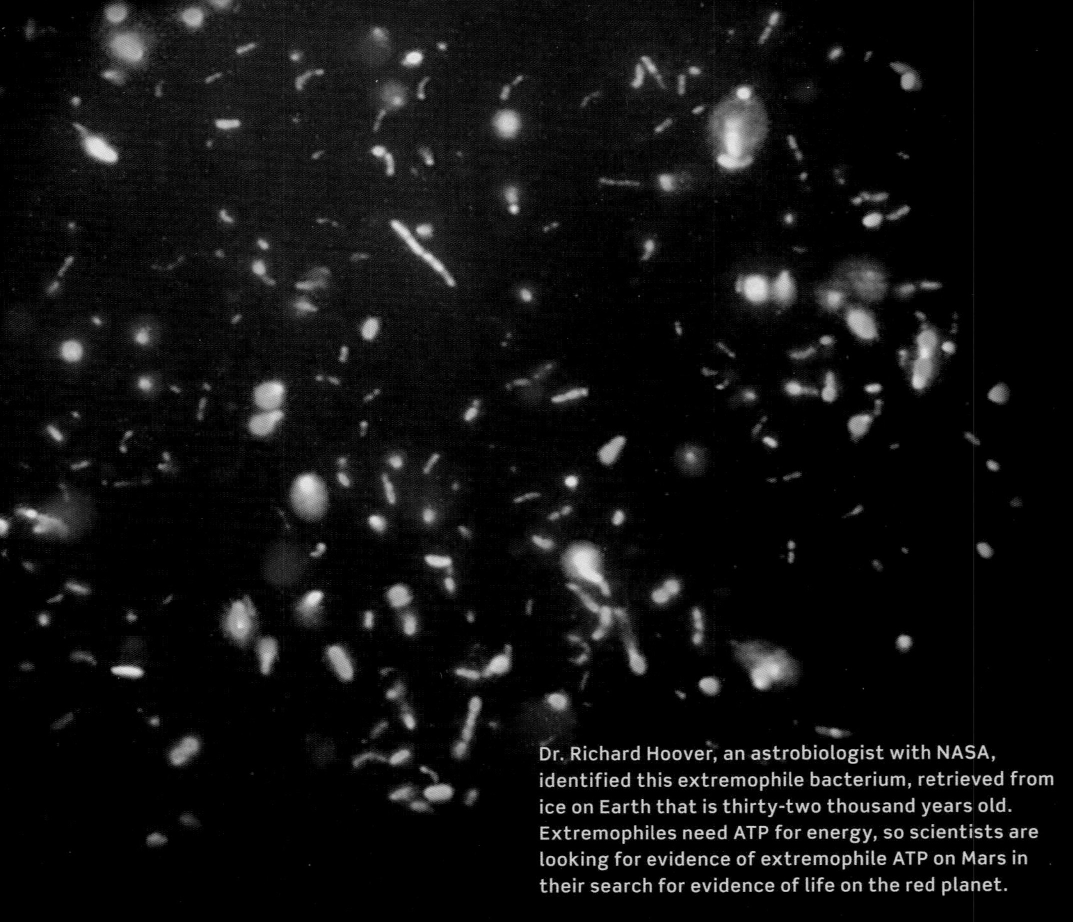

Dr. Richard Hoover, an astrobiologist with NASA, identified this extremophile bacterium, retrieved from ice on Earth that is thirty-two thousand years old. Extremophiles need ATP for energy, so scientists are looking for evidence of extremophile ATP on Mars in their search for evidence of life on the red planet.

heated water. Astrobiologists believe that the extremophiles living in the boiling, sulfurous waters near deep-sea hydrothermal vents on Earth may be similar to the organisms that might once have lived on Mars.

To detect evidence of extremophiles on Mars, scientists are relying on the fact that extremophiles use ATP as an energy source. Engineers have designed numerous instruments to help find traces of ATP on Mars. These instruments collect Martian soil, add a source of luciferin and luciferase, and scan for light before sending the information back to Earth. One of the main problems researchers face is making sure their ultrasensitive life-detection systems are able to distinguish between forms of life from Earth and those actually found in space. To make sure Mars missions do not bring ATP from Earth that could contaminate Martian samples, the American and European space agencies use firefly luciferase ATP tests to ensure that there is no ATP contamination before takeoff.

Quorum Sensing

Each human body is made up of about ten trillion cells, plus another ten trillion bacterial cells living inside or on the body. Bacteria help the immune system detect enemies, aid the digestive system in breaking down food, and help the body adjust vitamin production to meet our nutritional needs.

However, some bacteria make us sick. Scientists are working to better understand how such simple organisms can be so critical and so threatening to human life. In 1977 microbiologists working at the Scripps Institution of Oceanography in San Diego, California, got a very important first clue from the bioluminescent bacteria in the Hawaiian bobtail squid. It turns out that the bacteria living in the squid's photophores bioluminesce only when they have reached a certain number of bacteria in the light organs. Only when they have reached this critical mass do they all light up at once.

How do the bacteria know that they have the correct number of bacteria in the photophores to light up? Scientists have discovered that each bioluminescent bacteria releases a "Hi, I am here" molecule into the light organs. When the concentration of these molecules is high enough, the light-producing reactions start. This ability of bacteria to detect the "Hi, I am here" molecules is called quorum sensing. After scientists discovered quorum sensing among the bioluminescent bacteria in the Hawaiian bobtail squid, they discovered that all bacteria use quorum sensing.

Scientists were then able to determine that the bacteria that make us sick don't release their harmful toxins in the body until they have multiplied to sufficiently high numbers to fight off attacks from the body's immune system. They use quorum sensing to count how many friendly bacteria (of the same sick-making species) and how many unfriendly bacteria (of the immune system species) are in their environment. When the number of sick-making bacteria reaches critical mass, they release their toxins and the person becomes sick. When the immune system is able to overwhelm the sick-making bacteria with immune bacteria, the body begins to heal.

Scientists are using the Hawaiian bobtail squid's bioluminescent bacteria as a model system to further investigate quorum sensing. They hope to find ways to combat harmful bacteria in the human body by disrupting the bacterial quorum sensing. If they can do so, the bacteria would then become vulnerable to the human immune system from the moment they enter the host and be less likely to make the human host sick.

CHAPTER 5 BIO*fluorescence*

This photo montage shows some of the 180 species of biofluorescent fish in the world's oceans. Biofluorescence is a form of light emission that does not involve a reaction between chemicals. Instead, it is a process of exchange of high-energy (blue) light for lower energy (red and green) light.

When living organisms give off light as a result of internal chemical reactions, scientists refer to the phenomenon as bioluminescence. If it is dark enough outside, we can see this light with our human eyes. Biofluorescence, on the other hand, is only visible to fish and some other marine animals. More than 180 biofluorescent fish species are known to exist. They range from sharks to soles to sand stargazers and scorpion fishes.

In biofluorescence, a molecule absorbs high-energy light (typically blue light) and immediately returns it to the surroundings as lower-energy light (typically green and red light). The molecule immediately emits this lower-energy light, a phenomenon that scientists refer to as fluorescence.

Fish can see fluorescent colors because their eyes have a filter that removes blue light from their field of vision. The high-energy blues that excite the fluorescent molecules overwhelm the eyes'

BIOFLUORESCENCE VERSUS PHOSPHORESCENCE

Bioluminescent and fluorescent organisms give off light in very different ways. However, fluorescence and phosphorescence are very similar processes. In fluorescence, a molecule is excited (absorbs light energy) and immediately returns it to the surroundings as lower-energy light. In phosphorescence, a molecule absorbs light energy but returns it slowly. A phosphorescent glow continues even after the high-energy exciting light is removed. A fluorescent glow stops immediately if the high-energy light is removed.

ability to see the low-energy fluorescent colors, so by removing blue light, the filters allow the fish to see fluorescent reds and greens and yellows. Other marine species don't have a similar filter and will therefore see only the high-energy blue light and not the glowing greens and reds and yellows. Scientists and others who want to observe biofluorescence use intense blue flashlights to excite the biofluorescent molecules, and they film through blue light filters.

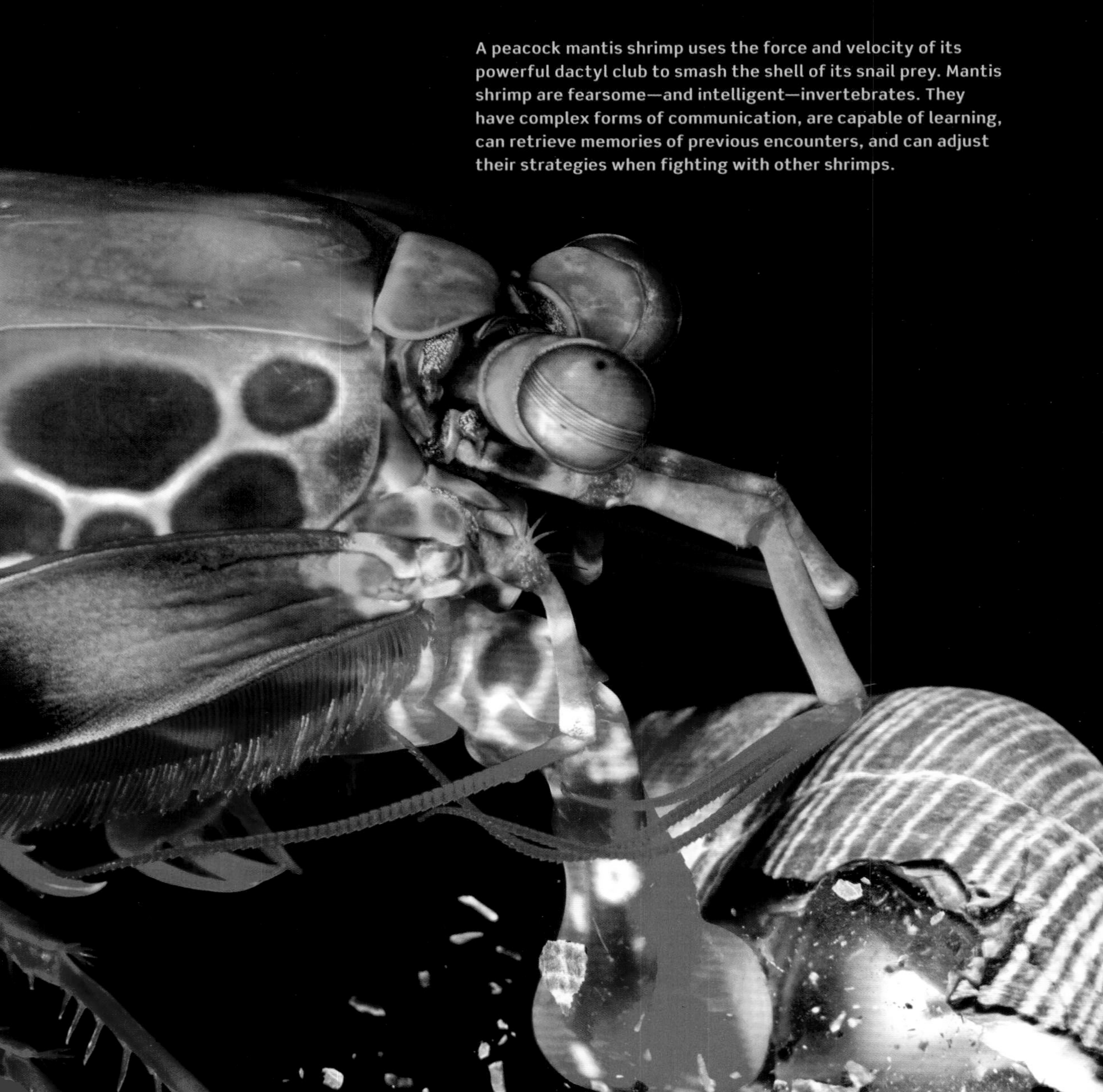

A peacock mantis shrimp uses the force and velocity of its powerful dactyl club to smash the shell of its snail prey. Mantis shrimp are fearsome—and intelligent—invertebrates. They have complex forms of communication, are capable of learning, can retrieve memories of previous encounters, and can adjust their strategies when fighting with other shrimps.

Biofluorescent Mantis Shrimp

Mantis shrimp, which live in burrows in shallow waters of the tropical oceans, are amazing creatures. They can shoot out their claws with the acceleration of a .22-caliber bullet and have the most advanced eyes known to exist in the animal kingdom. In several species of mantis shrimp, the males have strongly fluorescent yellow patches on their carapace (the upper part of the animal's exoskeleton, or outer shell).

Mantis shrimp can grow to be up to 1 foot (0.3 m) long, and marine biologists divide them into two groups, depending on how they attack their prey. Spearers pierce the fish they hunt with their claws. Smashers bludgeon crabs, snails, and mollusks. Male shrimp lack teeth and cannot immediately eat the food they catch, so they pass it on to the female. She masticates (chews) the food and passes it back to the male as an edible paste.

Male mantis shrimp are very territorial. But given their deadly claws, it is risky for mantis shrimp to fight each other. For this reason, they first judge the size of the fluorescent patches on a competitor's chest to decide whether it is worth challenging him. Large shrimp have large patches, and small shrimp have small patches. Only when males have similarly sized patches will they fight for a burrow, which often contains a potential mate. Otherwise, the mantis shrimp with the smaller fluorescent patch will always surrender. By painting larger fluorescent patches on smaller males, scientists in experimental settings have been able to change the ranking of the smaller males. They have found that a small mantis shrimp with a large fluorescent patch can rule the roost.

The mantis shrimp is also known for its remarkable eyes. They are positioned on flexible stalks on the animal's head to allow the shrimp to see in many directions.

Mantis shrimp have at least twelve different types of photoreceptors (a lens and sensory cells) in their eyes. Scientists suspect that the sophisticated eyes of the predatory mantis shrimp evolved to efficiently hunt fast-moving fish. The shrimp's eyes rapidly detect and distinguish among different-colored prey. The shrimp are not concerned with recognizing small differences in color. It is more important that they use their limited brain capacity to identify an edible fish, calculate the trajectory of that fish in a split second, and capture the prey before the fish sees the shrimp and swims away.

Crystal Jellyfish

If you happen to meet a jellyfish while swimming in the ocean, it's a good idea to get out of the way! Jellyfish, which live in all the oceans of the world, including the Arctic and the Southern Oceans, can sting an enemy or surprise a visitor with a neurotoxin released by the stinging cells that cover their tentacles. The most venomous jellyfish is the beautiful but deadly Australian sea wasp. If an Australian sea wasp stings a human being, that person can die in as few as three minutes if he or she doesn't get help immediately.

Some jellyfish have been observed at depths of more than 3,200 feet (975 m) below the surface of the water, and many types have been around since before the time of the dinosaurs. If all the water were squeezed out of a jellyfish, you wouldn't have much left over. A typical jellyfish is made up

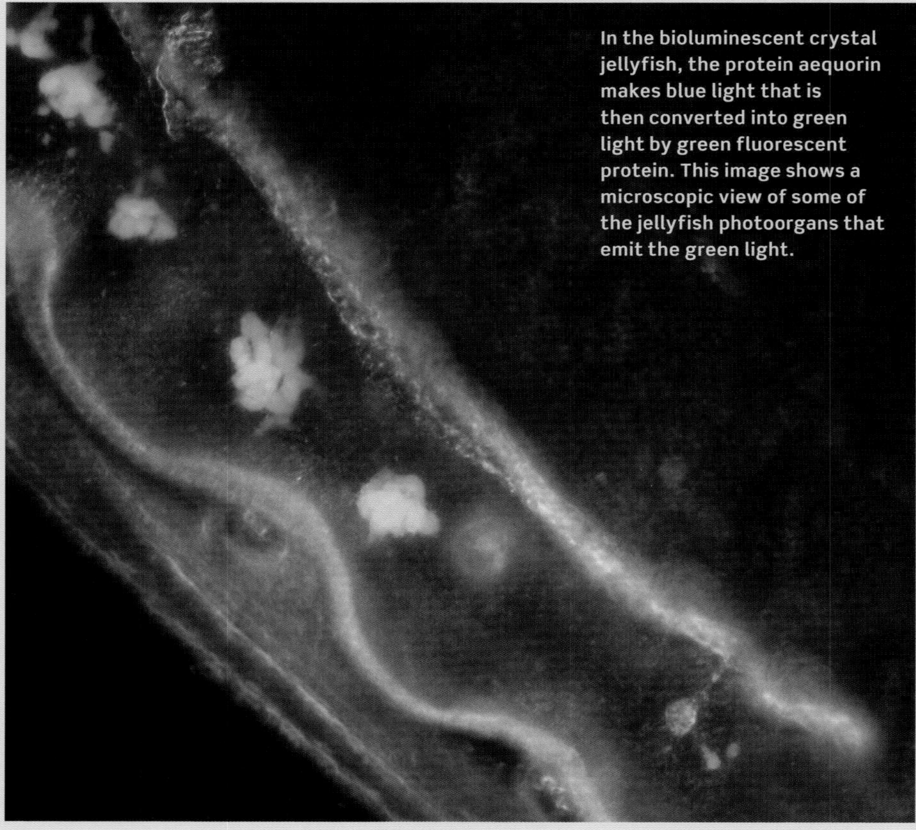

In the bioluminescent crystal jellyfish, the protein aequorin makes blue light that is then converted into green light by green fluorescent protein. This image shows a microscopic view of some of the jellyfish photoorgans that emit the green light.

of 96 percent water, 3 percent protein, and 1 percent minerals. They have no bones, hearts, or brains.

The umbrella of the crystal jellyfish does have an intriguing feature, however. It is marked with hundreds of photoorgans that emit pinpricks of green light. The organs only occasionally light up, and no one really knows why the jellyfish decides to turn them on.

If Guinness World Records had an entry for the person who has caught the most jellyfish in the world, Osamu Shimomura of Princeton University in New Jersey and Woods Hole Oceanographic Institution in Massachusetts would hold the title. He has caught more than one million crystal jellyfish. That is how many it took for him to figure out that all crystal jellyfish have two proteins involved in making light. One is aequorin. Shimomura named this protein after *Aequorea victoria*, the scientific name for the crystal jellyfish. The other is green fluorescent protein, which sits right next to aequorin in the jellyfish's photoorgans. When the jellyfish releases calcium, it binds with the aequorin and releases energy equivalent to blue light. The GFP then absorbs this energy and emits it as a green fluorescent light that is visible to the human eye.

CHAPTER 6

THE GREEN *Fluorescent* PROTEIN

The proteins responsible for biofluorescence are known as fluorescent proteins. Every cell in a fluorescent organism contains the genetic recipe, or code, for making fluorescent proteins. The recipe is in the form of deoxyribonucleic acid, or DNA. While at Princeton University, Osamu Shimomura discovered fluorescent proteins in crystal jellyfish in the 1960s. Since then scientists have found fluorescent proteins in more than 250 additional species.

Scientists have discovered that they can take the fluorescent protein genes from a biofluorescent organism, make millions of copies, and put them into any other animal's cells. When illuminated with blue light, the fluorescent protein will glow. Molecular biologists have done this with many animals, including mice, cats, and even monkeys.

Scientists do this because proteins are very small and are impossible to see in a cell or to track in a living organism without some form of technology as an aid. Fluorescent proteins give off visible light, and this light helps researchers detect the proteins. It's like seeing the light of a firefly at night even if you would be too far away to see the firefly itself during the day. This is incredibly useful because it allows scientists to observe what is happening at a subcellular level inside living organisms. From there, researchers can make advancements in the treatment of diseases and improve surgical techniques.

Scientists genetically modified these two monkeys by inserting the genes for fluorescent proteins from a jellyfish into their cells. By shining a blue light on the monkeys, they glow green. GFP research is allowing researchers to make amazing discoveries about diseases and life-threatening conditions with the goal of finding cures and treatments.

DNA, Genes, and GFP

The molecular machinery in the cell of a living organism uses instructions encoded in the DNA of the cell to make proteins. DNA is a sort of scientific cookbook that contains all the recipes required to make every kind of protein found in an organism's body. Scientists call the recipes genes. The complete set of instructions on how to make all the proteins in the body is called the genome. Humans are made up of

CLONING GFP

The GFP gene was first cloned in 1992 by Douglas Prasher at Woods Hole Oceanographic Institution in Massachusetts. He isolated the GFP gene from crystal jellyfish and inserted it into the DNA of bacteria, which expressed the GFP. In the twenty-first century, GFP is found in laboratories all over the world, where it is used to study a wide range of plants and animals. The importance of GFP was recognized in 2008 when the Nobel Committee awarded chemists Osamu Shimomura, Martin Chalfie, and Roger Tsien the Nobel Prize in Chemistry for the discovery and development of GFP.

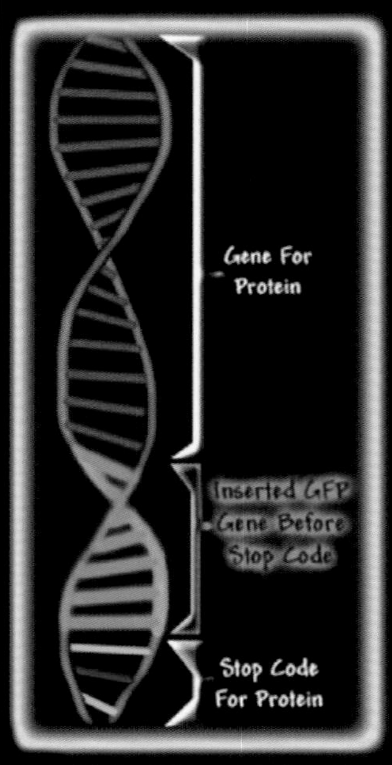

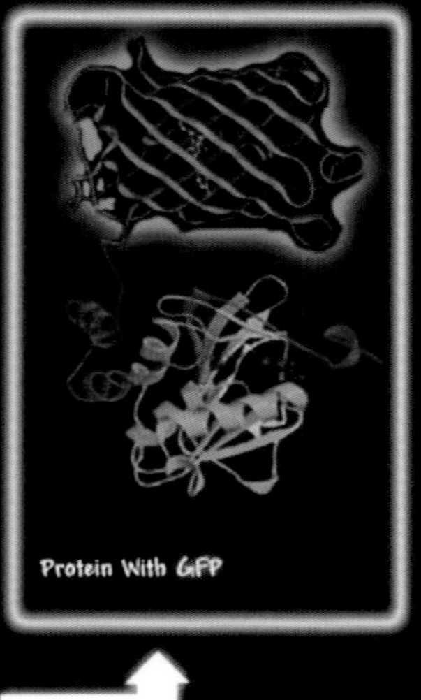

A gene is the portion of DNA that has the information required to make a protein. A stop codon signifies the end of the gene. The gene is the recipe describing how the protein is made. By inserting the GFP gene into the host's DNA so that it is located just before the stop codon, a new gene is created *(FAR LEFT)* that codes for a new protein fused with GFP *(NEAR LEFT)*. Shine a blue light on this protein and it will glow.

about ten trillion cells. Each cell has a nucleus, and in each nucleus is a complete set of instructions.

Using modern DNA technology, molecular biologists can use GFP in many arenas. For example, they can tag GFP onto hemoglobin, the oxygen-carrying protein in red blood cells. To do this, scientists use the DNA's index to direct the molecular machinery to the beginning of the hemoglobin gene sequence. When new hemoglobin is required, the machinery directs protein production by reading the DNA instructions. At the end of the gene is a genetic message called a stop codon, which ends protein production. It is the signal that says, "Stop, this is the end of the gene." The manufacture of proteins using the instructions from the gene is called protein expression.

Using these biomolecular techniques, scientists can insert the GFP gene at the end of the hemoglobin gene, right before the stop codon. Then, instead of stopping when the hemoglobin is made, the cell carries on making GFP, which becomes part of the hemoglobin. The process stops when the stop codon at the end of the GFP gene is reached. As a result, the cell produces a hemoglobin molecule with a GFP attached to it. The hemoglobin molecule is fluorescent. Using a fluorescence microscope, scientists can see where and when and how the hemoglobin is made. This has many important applications for scientists who are studying diseases associated with red blood cell disorders such as anemia and malaria. It is just one of the many exciting ways in which researchers are using GFP in twenty-first-century medical research.

CHAPTER 7

ILLUMINATING MODERN SCIENCE WITH *Fluorescent* PROTEINS

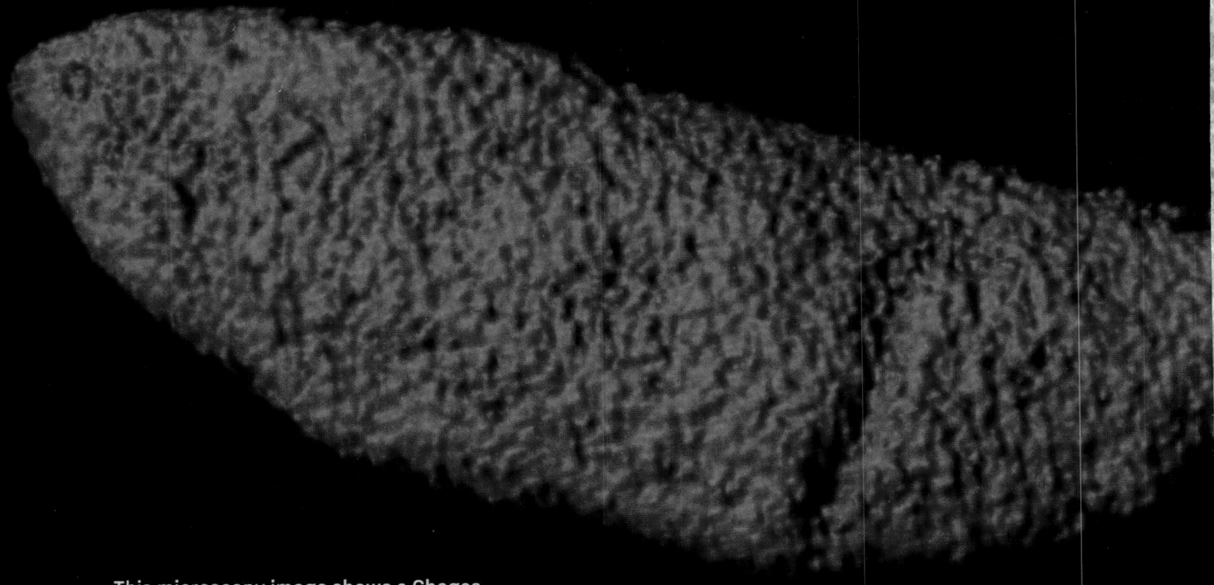

This microscopy image shows a Chagas parasite covered in red fluorescent proteins. The visibly glowing proteins allow researchers to follow the parasite inside a lab mouse to learn more about the transmission of Chagas disease.

Each year fluorescent proteins are used in millions of experiments, leading scientists of the twenty-first century to amazing new understandings, treatments, and technological advances. Thanks to fluorescent proteins, scientists can see when individual brain cells fire, learn more about how the human immunodeficiency virus (HIV) spreads so quickly, and make super-resolution fluorescent microscopes that allow for extremely clear, detailed, and high-quality imagery of subcellular life.

Chagas Disease

More than ten million people, mostly in Central America, have Chagas disease. The parasitic illness initially leads to fever, swollen lymph nodes, and body aches. If left untreated, about 30 percent of people with Chagas disease will develop deadly heart problems decades after the initial onset of the illness. Chagas is transmitted by Triatominae insects, also called kissing bugs. The insects often bite sleeping human victims on the face to feed off their blood. During their blood meal, the kissing bugs defecate near the bite wound. In infected insects, the feces contain a parasite called *Trypanosoma cruzi* (*T. cruzi*), which causes Chagas disease. The bites itch, and scratching the bites allows the parasites to enter their new host through the wound.

Parasitologists have created red fluorescent proteins that bind to the sugar molecules that cover the surface of *T. cruzi* parasites. The researchers clone bacteria that live in the kissing bug to express these fluorescent proteins. Then, using blue light and a fluorescent microscope, they can see the parasite growing and multiplying in the kissing bug's gut before it leaves the bug by its rear exit. Researchers have also followed the fluorescent *T. cruzi* parasites as

KISSING BUGS

Kissing bugs *(BELOW)* hide out in dark, protected places, such as cracks in the walls of poorly constructed homes or in thatch roofs. More than fourteen thousand kissing bugs can be found in a single chronically infested home. At night they leave their hiding spots and follow the plumes of carbon dioxide exhaled by their sleeping victims. Once they have found their victims, the kissing bugs unfold their tube-like proboscides (sucking mouthparts) and have a leisurely five- to ten-minute blood meal.

Charles Darwin was bitten by a kissing bug while traveling through Chile in 1835. He later contracted Chagas disease and described the original bite: "It is most disgusting to feel soft wingless insects about an inch [2.5 cm] long crawling over one's body. Before sucking they are quite thin, but after become round and bloated with blood."

they make their way around a mouse infected with the fluorescent bacteria through the kissing bug bite and feces. Thanks to the fluorescent parasites, scientists can tell how the parasite travels through the kissing bug's digestive tract, where it hides in the bug's body, and how it enters the host from the kissing bug's feces.

The most important characteristic of the red fluorescent *T. cruzi* is that they don't cause Chagas disease in the animals that are bitten by the infected kissing bugs. The sugar molecules that cover the parasite are bound up by the fluorescent proteins and cannot facilitate the entry of the parasite into a victim's cells.

Lighting Up the Brain

More than five million people in the United States are living with Parkinson's and Alzheimer's diseases. These are neurodegenerative diseases in which brain cells deteriorate and no longer function properly. This causes tremors, loss of memory, difficulty with speech, and muscle stiffness. There are currently no known cures for either disease.

As part of the search for treatments, neuroscientists led by Karel Svoboda at the Janelia Research Campus of the Howard Hughes Medical Institute in Virginia are learning more about how healthy brain cells work. They use a special group of mice into which they have inserted the GFP gene in all the nerve cells that go from the mice's whiskers to their brains. These same mice have also undergone a procedure to implant a glass window in the tops of their heads. Scientists set up microscopes at this window so they can watch the green fluorescence of the brain cells in action in the live mice.

A mouse relies on its whiskers as key sensory tools to navigate its environment. When the mouse is kept in a cage with little stimulation, where it can easily find its water and food, it doesn't use its whiskers much. Under these conditions, the mouse has very few brain cells connecting the whiskers to the brain. However, if the same mouse is placed in a maze, it has to use its whiskers much more to find its way through the space and to locate its meals. In this more challenging environment, the mouse's brain requires more information from the whiskers to navigate the space. The brain cells therefore branch out and form many new connections from the whiskers to the brain. In the GFP-modified mice, scientists can easily see what is happening to the brain cells associated with the whiskers because they are the only ones in the brain that glow green.

To watch mice adapt to compromised senses, scientists shave off all of a mouse's whiskers on one side of its face. The mouse must learn how to

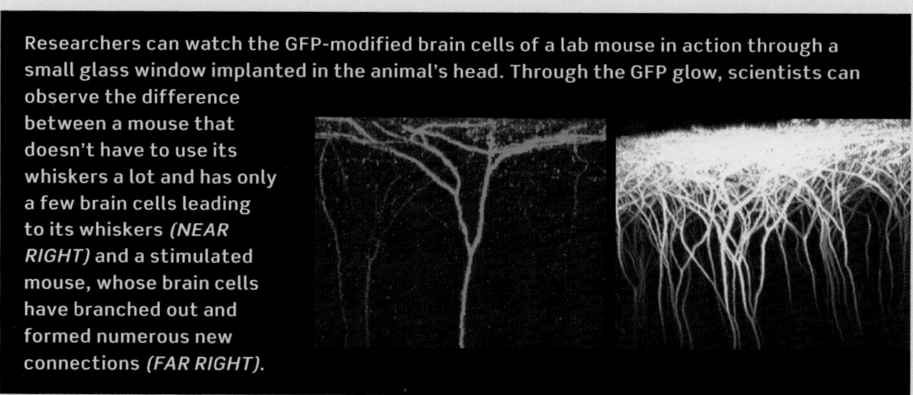

Researchers can watch the GFP-modified brain cells of a lab mouse in action through a small glass window implanted in the animal's head. Through the GFP glow, scientists can observe the difference between a mouse that doesn't have to use its whiskers a lot and has only a few brain cells leading to its whiskers *(NEAR RIGHT)* and a stimulated mouse, whose brain cells have branched out and formed numerous new connections *(FAR RIGHT)*.

find its way around the maze with just half its whiskers. By looking through the glass window, scientists can watch the GFP-labeled brain cells to see exactly how the mouse rewires its brain to do so. Scientists hope that by understanding how a mouse's brain adapts under compromised situations, we may one day figure out how to rewire compromised human brains. If we can do so, we may be able to effectively treat Parkinson's and Alzheimer's.

Influenza and Bird Flu

Seasonal influenza (flu) outbreaks occur all over the world, affecting millions of people every year. Flu symptoms are similar to cold symptoms, but they are more severe. At least four times in recorded history, a flu outbreak has swept across most of the world, infecting and killing a significant portion of its population. Such widespread outbreaks are known as pandemics.

The Spanish flu in 1918 was the world's worst pandemic. About one-third of the world's population was infected. People with this flu coughed and sneezed so violently that they tore the tissues of their lungs and burst their eardrums. Many patients bled from their eyes, noses, and every other orifice of the body. Historians estimate that between fifty and one hundred million people—more than 3 percent of the world's population at that time—died from the Spanish flu.

The 1918 flu was a zoonotic virus, a type of disease that jumps from one species to another. Historians think that the Spanish flu probably started in birds before passing through pigs to humans. The bird (or avian) flu still kills millions of chickens and ducks every year—mostly in Asian countries, where people live in close contact with fowl. Bird flu viruses can infect people who come in contact with birds, and they are the most deadly flu humans can get. So far, it has been impossible to eradicate the flu virus from wild birds or poultry farms or to prevent its transmission to other mammals, including humans.

The bird flu virus behaves differently in humans than in its native animal host. In humans, the virus attacks the lungs, but in birds, it infects the gastrointestinal tract and leads to diarrhea. As a consequence, bird droppings can harbor significant amounts of the avian virus and can contaminate lakes and ponds.

In research to combat the spread of bird flu, scientists have developed genetically modified chickens. The bird flu can infect these chickens, but the genetic modification prevents polymerase (an enzyme) from copying the flu virus's ribonucleic acid (RNA, a type of molecule very similar to DNA that carries all the virus's genetic information). The viruses therefore cannot multiply in the chickens, and so they do not infect other birds. All the genetically modified chickens also contain GFP, which means that the chickens that don't spread the bird flu are fluorescent. This makes them easy to distinguish and separate from the non-modified chickens.

Dengue Fever

The first descriptions of patients with symptoms like dengue fever were reported in a Chinese medical dictionary as early as 400 CE. Fever, pain in the eyeballs, and a rash are some of the common symptoms of this viral disease. If the disease—of which there are four types—progresses to the

The chick on the right has been genetically modified with GFP to distinguish it from non-modified chicks *(LEFT)*. It has also been modified to prevent it from transmitting the bird flu virus.

hemorrhagic stage, a person will suffer from oral and intestinal bleeding, which can be deadly.

In the twenty-first century, dengue fever, which is transmitted to humans by a bite of the *Aedes aegypti* mosquito, is the fastest-spreading disease in the world. About fifty to one hundred million people are infected with dengue fever in more than one hundred countries, making it twenty times more common than the flu.

Patients who have previously been infected with a dengue virus can get dengue hemorrhagic fever and dengue shock syndrome if they are infected again with a different type of dengue virus. The symptoms of hemorrhagic fever include persistent vomiting, severe abdominal pain, and difficulty breathing. This marks the beginning of a twenty-four- to forty-eight-hour period during which the body's smallest blood vessels become leaky, leading to failure of the circulatory system and to shock. If left untreated, 20 percent of the patients will die from the disease.

Medical science has not yet found a cure or developed a vaccine for dengue fever. The only way to control the spread of the disease is by limiting the spread of the *Aedes* mosquitoes. These mosquitoes bite during daylight hours and thrive in urban environments. They are stealthy stingers, they do not buzz like other mosquitoes, and they can bite as many as twenty people a day. Controlling and limiting the habitat of these mosquitoes is extremely difficult, as they can lay eggs in a single drop of water.

In Brazil, where dengue fever is very common, health authorities recently opened a new facility that can produce four million genetically modified fluorescent mosquitoes each week. At their larval life stage, the mosquitoes are sorted according to sex. Because only pregnant females bite humans, workers kill the females before releasing the males into the wild. The released males spend their lives searching for and mating with females in the area where they were freed. However, the genetically modified male mosquitoes carry a lethal gene that ties up the molecular machinery of their offspring. For this reason, all larva produced by the females who mated with the genetically modified males will die. If enough genetically modified males are released in a particular area, the *Aedes* mosquito population collapses.

The genetically modified mosquitoes, which are fluorescent, are easily distinguished from the wild mosquitoes. This allows the scientists

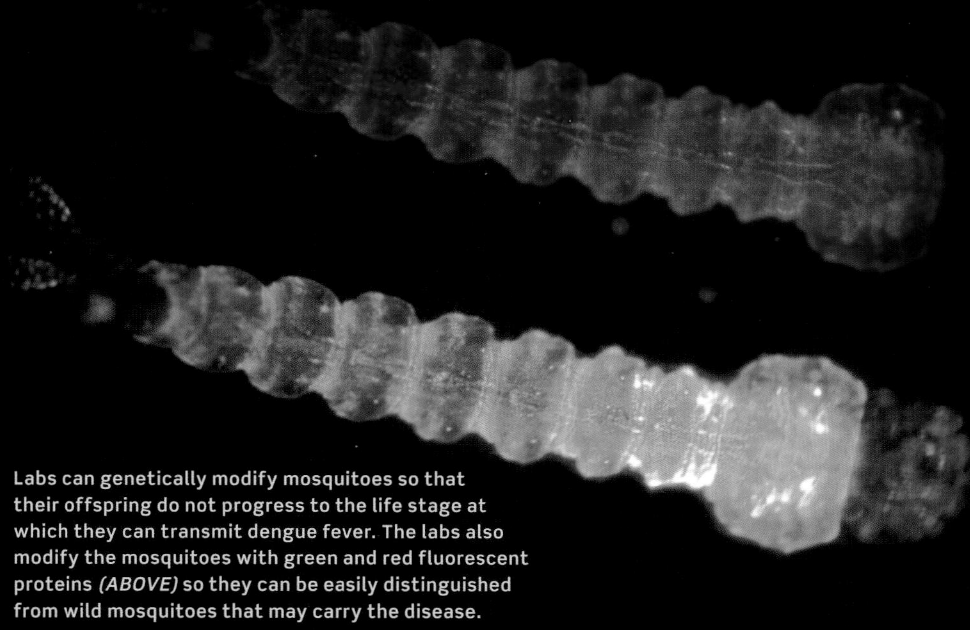

Labs can genetically modify mosquitoes so that their offspring do not progress to the life stage at which they can transmit dengue fever. The labs also modify the mosquitoes with green and red fluorescent proteins *(ABOVE)* so they can be easily distinguished from wild mosquitoes that may carry the disease.

monitoring the pest-control program to release just the right amount of genetically modified males to collapse the population and maximize the effectiveness of the program. The fluorescent mosquitoes have been released in the Brazilian city of Juazeiro. The program was a success there, with a decrease of more than 90 percent of *Aedes* mosquitoes. The program is being expanded to other cities in Brazil and is under consideration in the United States.

Malaria

Humans described the pain and suffering of malaria in Mesopotamian tablets crafted around six thousand years ago, in Sanskrit texts written about the ancient mythic Hindu surgeon Dhanvantari in 800 BCE, and in the writings of Shakespeare in the 1500s and the 1600s CE. The ancient Chinese knew that malarial fevers were associated with an enlarged spleen, and they blamed malaria's headaches, chills, and fevers on three demons: one carrying a hammer, a second a pail of water, and the third a hot stove.

In the twenty-first century, we know that malaria is caused by various malaria parasites of the *Plasmodium* genus and is transferred through the bite of infected female *Anopheles* mosquitoes. About three hundred to five hundred million people are infected with malaria each year in warm

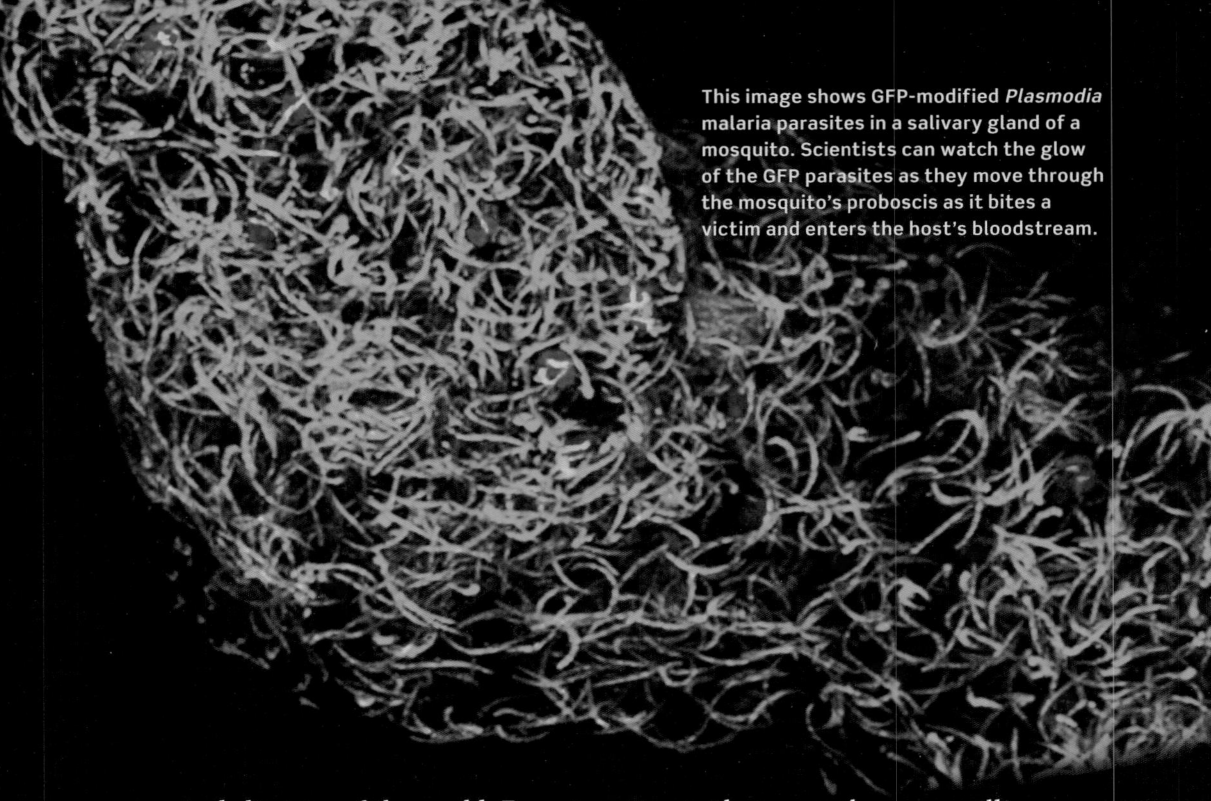

This image shows GFP-modified *Plasmodia* malaria parasites in a salivary gland of a mosquito. Scientists can watch the glow of the GFP parasites as they move through the mosquito's proboscis as it bites a victim and enters the host's bloodstream.

tropical climates of the world. Experts estimate that more than one million people, most of them in Africa, die annually from the disease.

When a female *Anopheles* mosquito infected with malaria parasites has a human blood meal, between twenty and one hundred parasites enter the human bloodstream. The malaria parasites are interested in hemoglobin, which is in the body's doughnut-shaped red blood cells and is responsible for the deep red color of blood.

Once in the human body, the *Plasmodium* races to the liver, an organ with few natural defenses. There, it builds up its forces and disguises itself before venturing back out into the bloodstream to infect the rest of the body.

To learn more about how the parasites protect themselves as they leave the liver and spread into red blood cells, researcher Robert Ménard and his team at the Pasteur Institute in Paris, France, genetically modified mice so that they had arteries lined with red fluorescent proteins. Then they infected the mice with a green fluorescent strain of *Plasmodium*.

By photographing the green glow of the *Plasmodium* in the bloodstream of the live mouse once every second, the team was able to record the parasites' trickery. The team discovered that before the parasites leave the liver, they enter dying liver cells that the body then

SICKLE CELL ANEMIA AND MALARIA

Up to 40 percent of the inhabitants of parts of Africa and South Asia have an inherited genetic mutation in their red blood cells called the sickle cell mutation that protects them from the malaria parasite. The mutation causes the red blood cells to collapse when attacked by the malaria parasite. The cells lose their doughnut shape and become rigid and crescent-shaped, making them impenetrable to the malaria parasite. For this reason, people with the sickle cell mutation are protected from malaria.

However, the mutation also causes a disease known as sickle cell anemia in which the irregular shape of the blood cells blocks the flow of blood in the body's limbs and organs, causing pain and damage to the organs. If both parents have the sickle cell mutation, offspring have a one in four chance of inheriting a copy of the mutated gene from each parent. The disorder was once deadly, but medical treatments are now available for individuals with sickle cell anemia, and having two copies of the gene is no longer fatal.

sheds into the bloodstream. Heavily disguised, the malaria parasites invade the red blood cells, where they feast on the hemoglobin and multiply until there is no room for anything else in the cells. Then all the infected red blood cells burst at the same time, releasing waves of parasites that move on to find new hemoglobin-laden red blood cells to take over. And the parasites excrete all their waste products into the captured red blood cells, which spew toxins and other waste products when they rupture. This is not good for the health of the human host, who can experience fever, headaches, nausea, and total misery every time a new generation of parasites is released with the waste of its predecessors. Through GFP research, medical experts hope to find a way to knock out the parasite's ability to take over dying liver cells.

Cancer

When healthy cells multiply, they follow a highly regulated process. Cancer cells are different. They grow and multiply without any controls and metastasize (spread) to other parts of the body. All cancers can infiltrate and then destroy normal body tissues. As one aspect of designing new anticancer drugs, researchers are working to better understand how cancer cells spread and invade parts of the body. In 1997 researchers at AntiCancer Inc. genetically modified human cancer cells with fluorescent proteins. The proteins allow scientists to follow the cells as they form a tumor in a lab mouse, break away from the tumor, and travel in the mouse's blood and lymphatic system before forming new tumors elsewhere in the animal's body. Thanks to GFP technology, this is the first time researchers have been able to follow tumor formation and metastasis in real time in live model organisms.

To grow and spread, cancer cells need oxygen and nutrients. Cancerous tumors get their essential nutrients from blood vessels formed from neighboring healthy tissue. This process of forming new blood vessels is called angiogenesis. AntiCancer Inc. has studied angiogenesis by implanting red fluorescent tumors into mice in which every cell expresses GFP. In live mice, the scientists can then follow the green fluorescent blood vessels growing into the red fluorescent tumors. These experiments are routinely used to test angiogenesis inhibitors, drugs designed to stop new blood vessels from entering tumors, thereby causing the cancers to shrink and die.

Limb Loss

Approximately 1.7 million people in the United States are living with the loss of one or more limbs. Such loss may be due to accidents or wartime injuries. However, it is most often due to diseases, such as diabetes, that affect the flow of blood through the body's blood vessels. As the blood flow becomes increasingly compromised, limbs such as the legs lose their vital supply of blood and become more vulnerable to infection. In extreme cases, the legs must be surgically amputated.

Doctors fit humans who have lost limbs with prosthetic legs. But the axolotl, a type of salamander found in lakes near Mexico City, Mexico, has the ability to regrow injured or missing parts of its body. If it loses a leg, it will regenerate another perfect one. If a piece of its lung is damaged, it can even grow new lung tissue.

Scientists want to know how the axolotls do this. To learn more about the champion axolotl regenerators, German researchers inserted jellyfish GFP into axolotl stem cells. Scientists know the stem cells play a key role in the axolotl regeneration process. Scientists then implant the axolotl GFP

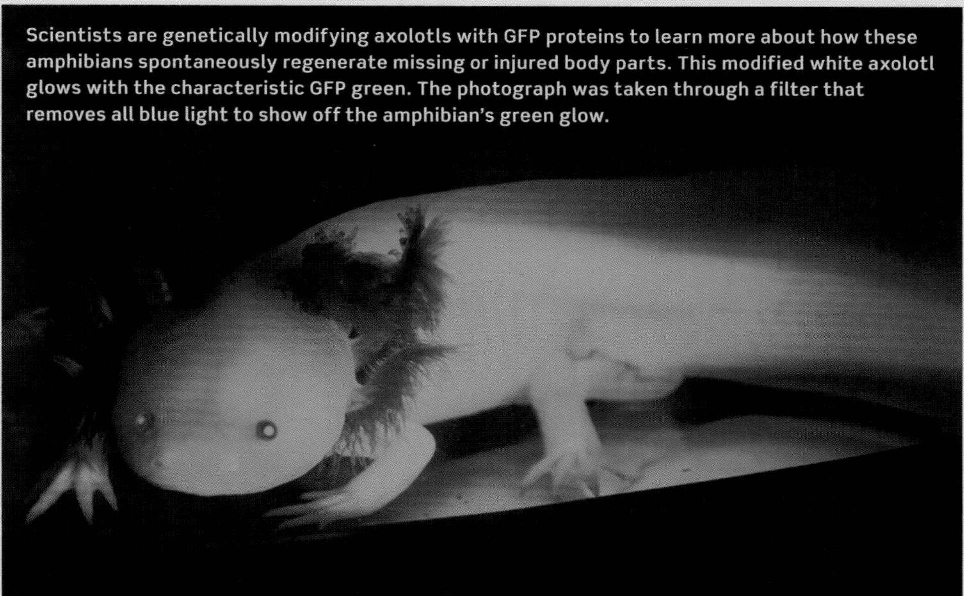
Scientists are genetically modifying axolotls with GFP proteins to learn more about how these amphibians spontaneously regenerate missing or injured body parts. This modified white axolotl glows with the characteristic GFP green. The photograph was taken through a filter that removes all blue light to show off the amphibian's green glow.

stem cells into an injured salamander. (Salamanders are closely related to axolotls.) If the axolotl stem cells function in the salamander, helping it repair its injuries, then the new tissue made from the axolotl stem cells in the salamander glows green. Other tissues formed by the salamander itself in other parts of its body don't give off any light, however. In this way, scientists can observe how the GFP axolotl cells work on the injured salamander cells. Researchers hope to figure out more precisely how the axolotls regenerate injured cells and even full limbs. From there, they might be able to help humans do the same thing if they have nerve damage or lose a limb or an organ through injury or disease.

Heart Disease

A healthy heart is key to life. But a range of health problems such as infections, diseases of the blood vessels, arrhythmia, and congenital defects can seriously weaken the heart. In fact, heart diseases are among the leading causes of death in many countries, including the United States, Canada, England, and Japan.

For a heart to beat, the organ requires oxygen to convert the high-energy molecules of ATP to energy in the heart muscles. Coronary arteries

STEM CELLS

Stem cells can be thought of as the seeds of regeneration, or new organ growth, in all animal life. When a stem cell divides, it has the ability either to remain a nonspecialized stem cell or to change into a cell with a more specialized function, such as a heart muscle cell or a brain cell. In growth before and shortly after birth, embryonic stem cells can differentiate (change) into any type of cell that the growing embryo needs.

In adults the function of the stem cells is to repair damaged organs. However, the stem cells' ability to differentiate into a variety of cell types is much more limited in adult animals. For example, liver stem cells can only become certain cells used in the liver. They can't become cells for the eyes or any other organ besides the liver. With GFP, researchers are able to track stem cells to learn more about how they move, multiply, and differentiate into other cell types.

supply the heart muscles with oxygen-laden blood. Blockages of these blood vessels can reduce the blood supply to the heart muscles, especially during times of stress and exertion when the heart needs more oxygen.

If the flow of blood to a section of a heart muscle is suddenly blocked, that part of the heart muscle is deprived of oxygen. The muscle's energy levels begin to fall, and the muscle itself may stop contracting. This is a heart attack. If the blockage (normally a blood clot) is not removed in a timely manner, oxygen deprivation occurs and the heart cells die. Cell death is halted when oxygenated blood begins to flow back into the affected areas. A mammal's heart has little capacity to regenerate, and the body usually replaces injured heart cells with scar tissue. Scar tissue does not contract, so the heart's ability to beat is weakened.

The fact that women in the last few months of pregnancy have the highest rate of recovery from heart failure piqued Hina Chaudhry's interest. She is an associate professor of myocardial regeneration at Mount Sinai School of Medicine in New York City. She wondered whether the stem cells of the child's developing heart were attracted to the injured maternal heart to do repair.

Using fluorescent proteins in a lab setting, Chaudhry has shown that if pregnant mice have a heart attack, embryonic stem cells cross the mother's umbilical cord and move to the injured maternal heart. There, the stem cells, which are genetically programmed to change into a variety of cell types, can change into different heart muscle cells. In her experiments on mice, Chaudhry used GFP-expressing male mice to impregnate nonfluorescent virgin female mice. Half the embryos from this mating were fluorescent. In healthy pregnant and postnatal (post-birthing) female mice, the mother's heart cells were not fluorescent. However, if the heart of the pregnant mouse was injured by a heart attack, Chaudhry observed new green fluorescent heart cells in the injured areas of the mouse's heart.

This is a stunning result. It implies that the heart sends out a chemical distress signal after a heart attack indicating that the heart needs stem cells. In women who have a heart attack in late stages of pregnancy, the same process is at work. The embryo responds by sending lifesaving embryonic stem cells to the source of the chemical distress signal (the heart) that then differentiate into the required heart cells. Chaudhry and other researchers hope to use this knowledge to learn how to differentiate stem cells into heart cells that can be implanted into sick humans to replace injured heart muscle cells.

Human Immunodeficiency Virus (HIV)

HIV is a cone-shaped virus that is much larger than the influenza or dengue viruses. The HIV virus is coated in sugars. These sugars are the key that HIV uses to get into the CD4+T cells (white blood cells) of an infected individual. All cells require energy to function, and sugars are an excellent source of this energy. When an HIV virus covered in sugar molecules comes along, the white cell membrane opens up and ingests the "food." Once inside the cell, the virus rests. One of the great difficulties in curing a patient with HIV is that the virus undergoes long periods of latency (inactivity). The virus only becomes active if and when the white blood cells are required to fight an infection. Then the HIV virus multiplies very rapidly and hijacks new CD4+T cells.

One of the questions that has plagued HIV researchers is how the newly released HIV cells so quickly find new CD4+T cells to hijack.

Researchers are using GFP to learn more about how HIV (red, in this image) spreads through the body.

By infecting a CD4+T cell with HIV containing GFP-labeled proteins, molecular immunologist Daniel Davis and his colleagues at Imperial College in London were able to show that HIV proteins travel down a sticky strand that is formed when two human T cells bump into each other. Davis has called these HIV highways membrane nanotubes. They can connect two T cells that are several cell lengths apart.

According to Davis, his data shows that "T-cell nanotubes are [new] physical connections between T cells that can have important consequences for allowing rapid spread of HIV-1 [a form of the HIV virus]. As the ability of HIV-1 to spread between cells is [key to its ability to cause disease], this mechanism of HIV-1 transmission . . . may open new avenues for drug targets."

What Will We Light Up Next?

The crystal jellyfish, with its green fluorescent proteins, has been floating around in the ocean for more than five hundred million years. In the 1990s, no one knew about fluorescent proteins. They have since become the new microscope of the twenty-first century. They allow us to see things we have never been able to see before. And like the actual microscope, they have completely changed the way we think about science and medicine.

We can watch as fluorescent malaria parasites travel from an infected mosquito into a mouse while it is being bitten. Fluorescent proteins have become invaluable tools to track HIV, to design chickens that are resistant to bird flu, and to confirm the existence of cancerous stem cells.

Who knows what bioluminescent and biofluorescent organisms will end up teaching us next? Mind reading and mind control are not out of the question. Using modified fluorescent proteins that light up when individual neurons fire in the brain, researchers at the Janelia Research Campus of the Howard Hughes Medical Institute in Virginia are getting very close to being able to read the minds of mice. Neurobiologists at Stanford University in California and at Massachusetts Institute of Technology in Cambridge are using this information to turn on the very same neurons by shining a blue light on them. Through this process, they will be able to control the minds of their genetically modified mice and direct the mice to do specific tasks. Science and nature are working together through these and other glowing technologies to push the boundaries of twenty-first-century science in new and exciting directions.

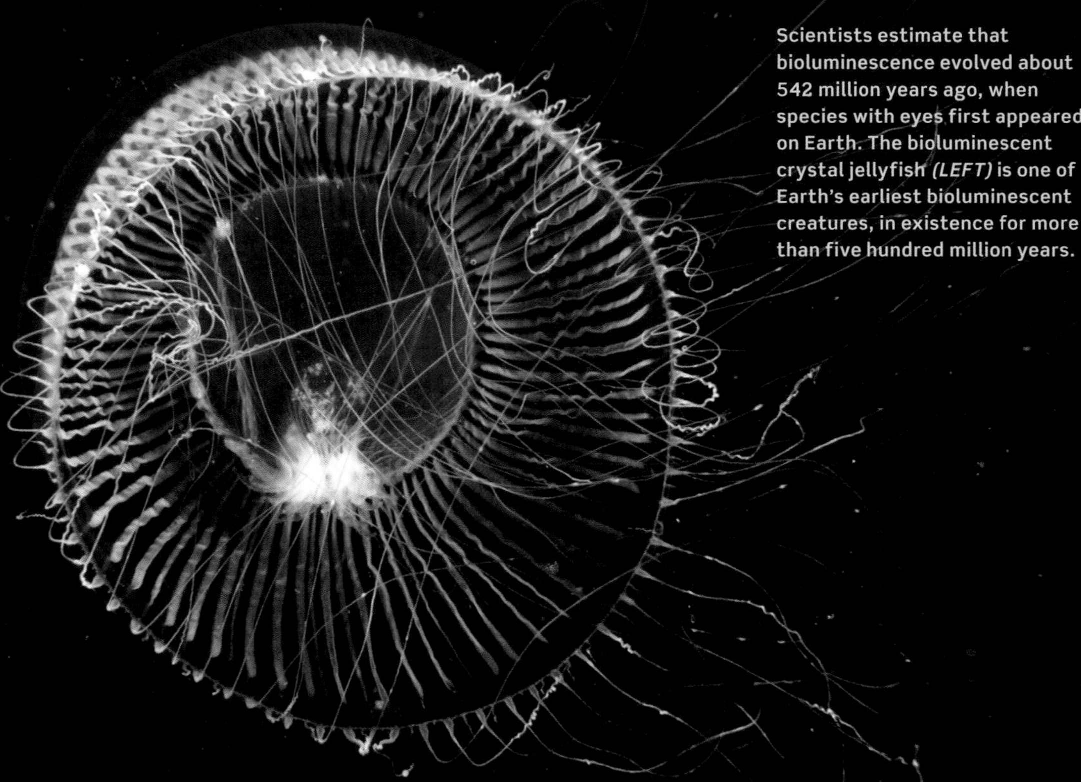

Scientists estimate that bioluminescence evolved about 542 million years ago, when species with eyes first appeared on Earth. The bioluminescent crystal jellyfish *(LEFT)* is one of Earth's earliest bioluminescent creatures, in existence for more than five hundred million years.

GLOSSARY

adenosine triphosphate (ATP): a molecule that is used to transfer energy throughout an organism. All living organisms, whether plant or animal, have ATP.

agar plate: a petri dish containing agar, a nutrient growth medium. It is often used for growing bacteria.

bacteriogenic bioluminescence: the chemical production and emission of light by bacteria living in a mutually beneficial, symbiotic relationship with their host

biofluorescence: the absorption of light and its immediate reemission as lower-energy light of a different color by living organisms

bioluminescence: the production and emission of light by living organisms through chemical processes

cold light: a form of light in which very little energy is lost as heat. Bioluminescence is a type of cold light.

color spectrum: the portion of the electromagnetic spectrum that can be seen by the human eye. Also known as the visible spectrum, it ranges from low-energy red light to high-energy violet light.

counter-illumination: the use of bioluminescence on the underside of a fish or a squid to match the light intensity of the water above the animal. Counter-illumination is a form of camouflage.

deoxyribonucleic acid (DNA): a molecule in which hereditary information is stored. It encodes the genetic instructions for all proteins in all living organisms.

electroluminescence: the emission of light in response to the passage of electric current

enzymes: large biological molecules (proteins) that speed up chemical reactions without being used up

gene: a unit of DNA that codes for a specific protein. Humans have approximately twenty-five thousand genes, while fruit flies have about thirteen thousand.

green fluorescent protein (GFP): a glowing protein discovered in jellyfish in 1961 by chemist and marine biologist Osamu Shimomura. The function of this protein in jellyfish is not known. Living organisms can be genetically modified with GFP to see where, when, and how proteins are made, where they go, and what functions they serve. Scientists hope GFP will lead to new treatments and drugs to fight disease.

larva: the newly hatched, wingless, feeding, and often wormlike life stage in the life cycle of insects and amphibians

lucibufagin: a defensive steroid emitted by male fireflies. Lucibufagin makes the fireflies distasteful to birds and spiders.

luciferase: an enzyme that, in combination with luciferin and oxygen, is responsible for bioluminescence. It was discovered and named by Raphaël Dubois in 1885.

luciferin: a small molecule that, in conjunction with luciferase and oxygen, makes the light of bioluminescence

phosphorescence: the absorption of light followed by the gradual reemission of light into the atmosphere

photocytes: the cells in which the luciferin/luciferase reaction of bioluminescence occurs

photophore: a collection of photocytes that maximizes the amount of light emitted by the photocytes; also known as a photoorgan

photoreceptor: a photosensitive cell in the retina of vertebrate eyes

proteins: large biological molecules that do most of the work in cells. They are responsible for the structure, functioning, and regulation of cells in all life-forms.

quorum sensing: the use of signaling molecules ("Hi, I am here" molecules) by bacteria to communicate and coordinate their behavior through the ability to detect the number of bacteria in any given space

ribonucleic acid (RNA): a molecule similar to DNA in which many viruses encode their genetic information

stem cell: an unspecialized cell that can differentiate into (become) a specific specialized cell, such as a heart or a muscle cell

super-resolution microscopy: techniques based on fluorescent proteins that allow microscopes to image objects smaller than half the wavelength of light. From 1873 to 2000, scientists believed it was impossible to see something so small with light. Biophysicists Eric Betzig, Stefan Hell, and William Moerner were awarded the 2014 Nobel Prize in Chemistry for their work in developing super-resolution microscopy.

symbiosis: a relationship between two organisms of different species that may but does not always benefit both organisms

ultraviolet light: the portion of the electromagnetic spectrum with shorter wavelengths (more energy) than visible light and longer wavelengths (less energy) than X-rays

virus: a small infectious agent that only replicates inside the living cells of other organisms. Viruses are typically made up of a protein coat that surrounds a core of genetic material (RNA or DNA).

zoonotic disease: a disease that can be transmitted between animals and humans

SOURCE NOTES

19 Benjamin Franklin, *Memoirs of the Life and Writings of Benjamin Franklin* (Philadelphia: W. Duane, 1809), 3:111.

19 Benjamin Franklin, *Memoirs of the Life and Writings of Benjamin Franklin* (Philadelphia: McCarthy & Davis, 1840), 2:355.

20 Aristotle, *Historia animalium*, trans. R. Creswell (London: Bell & Sons, 1887), n.p.

20 Pliny the Elder, *Natural History*, trans. H. Rackham (Cambridge, MA: Harvard University Press, 1940), 3:467.

21 Ibid., 287.

50 Charles Darwin, *Journal of Researches into the Natural History and Geology of the Countries Visited during the Voyage of H.M.S.* "Beagle" *Round the World* (London: John Murray, 1882), 333.

52 S. Sowinski, C. Jolly, O. Berninghausen, M. A. Purbhoo, A. Chauveau, K. Kohler, S. Oddos, P. Eissmann, F. M. Brodsky, C. Hopkins, B. Onfelt, Q. Sattentau, and D. M. Davis, "Membrane Nanotubes Physically Connect T Cells over Long Distances Presenting a Novel Route for HIV-1 Transmission," *Nature Cell Biology* 10 (February 2008): 211–219.

SELECTED BIBLIOGRAPHY

Haddock, S. H. D., M. A. Moline, and J. F. Case. "Bioluminescence in the Sea." *Annual Review of Marine Science* 2 (2010): 443–493.

Harvey, E. Newton. *A History of Luminescence from the Earliest Times until 1900.* Philadelphia: American Philosophical Society, 1957.

Pieribone, V. A., and D. F. Gruber. *Aglow in the Dark: The Revolutionary Science of Biofluorescence.* Cambridge, MA: Belknap, 2005.

Widder, E. A. "Bioluminescence in the Ocean: Origins of Biological, Chemical, and Ecological Diversity." *Science* 328 (2010): 704–708.

Widder, E. A., and B. Falls. "Review of Bioluminescence for Engineers and Scientists in Biophotonics." *IEEE Journal of Selected Topics in Quantum Electronics* 20, no. 2 (2014): 1–10

Wilson, Thérèse, and J. Woodland Hastings. *Bioluminescence: Living Lights, Lights for Living.* Cambridge, MA: Harvard University Press, 2013.

Zimmer, Marc. *Glowing Genes: A Revolution in Biotechnology.* Amherst, NY: Prometheus, 2005.

FOR FURTHER INFORMATION

BOOKS

Johnson, Rebecca L. *Journey into the Deep: Discovering New Ocean Creatures.* Minneapolis: Millbrook Press, 2011. In this award-winning book for young readers, Johnson explores the amazing results of the Census of Marine Life, completed in 2010, and discusses bioluminescent creatures among the ocean's diverse life-forms.

Sitarski, Anita. *Cold Light: Creatures, Discoveries, and Inventions That Glow.* Honesdale, PA: Boyds Mills, 2007. Written for a middle school audience, this book reviews the history of bioluminescence and the invention of many nonbioluminescent objects such as glow sticks and LED bulbs.

Zimmer, Marc. *Illuminating Disease: An Introduction to Green Fluorescent Proteins.* New York: Oxford University Press, 2015. Written by the author of this book, *Illuminating Disease* describes how fluorescent proteins can be used to examine diseases such as HIV/AIDS, cancer, malaria, influenza, and dengue fever.

WEBSITES

The Bioluminescence Web Page

http://biolum.eemb.ucsb.edu/

This reliable website about marine bioluminescence is maintained by marine biologist Steven Haddock at the Monterey Bay Aquarium Research Institute in Monterey, California. The site has sections on questions, myths, functions, organisms, photos, chemistry, physiology, and research—all related to bioluminescence.

GFP

http://www.conncoll.edu/ccacad/zimmer/GFP-ww/GFP-1.htm

Hosted by Marc Zimmer, the GFP site is designed for students and teachers who are interested in green fluorescent proteins and all their uses. The site has sections on GFP history, the 2008 Nobel Prize in Chemistry for the discovery of GFP, natural history, cool uses of GFP, and GFP structure.

Luminescent Labs

http://www.luminescentlabs.org/science.html

With some information about bioluminescence, this site's main focus is marine biofluorescence. It is hosted by natural history experts David Gruber and John Sparks of the American Museum of Natural History in New York. The site has sections that investigate bioluminescent life, biofluorescent life, and biofluorescent corals

SHORT VIDEOS

"Amazing and Weird Creatures Exhibit Bioluminescence—Blue Planet." YouTube video, 2:18. Posted by "BBC Earth," May 18, 2009. http://www.youtube.com/

watch?v=UXl8F-eIoiM. This preview of the BBC televsion series *The Blue Planet* is narrated by Sir David Attenborough. It includes footage of anglerfish and other bioluminescent fish.

"Bioluminescence on Camera." National Geographic TV, 3:56. http://channel.nationalgeographic.com/channel/videos/bioluminescence-on-camera In this short documentary, viewers learn how scientists use light-sensitive startlight cameras in the Caribbean Sea to film bioluminescent squid and dinoflagellates.

"Blinded by the Light." YouTube video, 0:34. Posted by "*NOVA* PBS," July 2, 2008. http://www.youtube.com/watch?v=6n8fCuDwn74. This very short video from the PBS television series *NOVA* shows a fire-breathing shrimp using bioluminescent slime as a defense mechanism.

"Superhero Science—Limb Regeneration." *Science Channel*. YouTube video, 2:17. Posted by "Science Channel," November 22, 2010. http://www.youtube.com/watch?v=EsCSwVx3GvA#t=38. This clip describes work done with axolotls at the leg laboratory at the University of California at Irvine.

TED Talks

Bassler, Bonnie. "How Bacteria 'Talk'." Filmed February 2009. TED video. 18:14. http://www.ted.com/talks/bonnie_bassler_on_how_bacteria_communicate?language=en. Bonnie Bassler is a professor of molecular biology and also a MacArthur Genius Award winner. In this talk, Bassler describes how bacteria that live in the Hawaiian bobtail squid communicate and light up only when the bacteria reach a certain density.

Widder, Edith. "Glowing Life in an Underwater World." Filmed April 2010. TED video, 17:19. http://www.ted.com/talks/edith_widder_glowing_life_in_an_underwater_world. Edith Widder is the world's premier bioluminescence expert. In 2006 she was awarded a MacArthur Genius Award. Here she talks about some of her work in the field of bioluminescence.

———. "How We Found the Giant Squid." Filmed February 2013. TED video, 8:38. http://www.ted.com/talks/edith_widder_how_we_found_the_giant_squid. Edith Widder describes how a bioluminescent lure was used to find and film a giant squid.

———. "The Weird, Wonderful World of Bioluminescence." Filmed March 2011. Ted video, 12:45. http://www.ted.com/talks/edith_widder_the_weird_and_wonderful_world_of_bioluminescence. Edith Widder talks about more of her work in the field of bioluminescence.

Zimmer, Marc. "Surfing the Fluorescent Wave." YouTube video, 11:39. Posted by "TEDx Talks," May 10, 2013. https://www.youtube.com/watch?v=XK1Ubcac5Mg. Marc Zimmer describes how fluorescent mice can be used to show that embryonic stem cells may fix damaged heart muscles in pregnant women who suffer a heart attack.

INDEX

PHOTO ACKNOWLEDGMENTS

The images in this book are used with the permission of: © Jurgen Freund/naturepl.com, p. 2; © Doug Perrine/SeaPics.com, p. 3 (bottom); © E. Widder/HBOI/Visuals Unlimited, Inc., p. 4; © Dr. Dennis Kunkel/Joe Scott/Visuals Unlimited, Inc., p. 5 (all); Mike Lewinski/ Wikimedia Commons (CC BY 2.0), pp. 6–7; © Laura Westlund/Independent Picture Service, pp. 9, 10, 14; © Masa Ushioda/age fotostock/SuperStock, pp. 12–13; © Eddie Widder, p. 15; © Eric Roettinger/Kahi Kai Images, p. 16; © Wim van Egmond/Visuals Unlimited, Inc., p. 18; © Freer Gallery of Art, Smithsonian Institution, USA/Robert O. Muller Collection/ Bridgeman Images, p. 21; © E. Widder/HBOI/Visuals Unlimited, Inc., p. 23; © Norbert Wu/ Minden Pictures/Getty Images, p. 24; © Sonke Johnsen/Visuals Unlimited/CORBIS, p. 25; © Trevor Williams/Taxi Japan/Getty Images, pp. 26–27; © E.R. Degginger/Alamy, p. 28; © tomosang/Moment/Getty Images, p. 29; © Photo by Werner Wolff/The LIFE Images Collection/Getty Images, p. 30; © Tsunemi Kubodera/The Royal Society via Copyright Clearance Center, p. 32; Courtey of Eddie Widder, p. 33; © Hunter Cole/Microbial Art/ Science Source, p. 34; Photo Courtesy Of Asim Bej/University of Alabama at Birming via NASA, p. 36; © David Gruber/John Sparks , pp. 38–39; © Roy Caldwell, p. 39; © S. Haddock/biolum.eemb.ucsb.edu, p. 42; © Yerkes National Primate Research Center/Emory University, pp. 44–45; © Marc Zimmer, p. 46; © Anatoliy Markiv, Bernard Anani, Ravi V. Durvasula, Angray S. Kang/Journal ofImmunological Methods/Elsevier via Copyright Clearance Center, pp. 48–49; © John Cancalosi/Alamy, p. 50; © Brian Chen and Karel Svoboda, Cold Spring Harbor Laboratory, p. 51;© Helen Sang/The Roslin Institute and R(D) SVS/University of Edinburgh, p. 53; Oxitec Limited (copyright 2011), p. 55; © Dr. Carina Gomes-Santos, p. 56; © Justin Rosenberg, p. 59; © CNRI/Science Photo Library/Getty Images, p. 62; © Hiroya Minakuchi/Minden Pictures, p. 63. **Front cover:** © E. Widder/ HBOI/Visuals Unlimited, Inc. **Back cover:** © Denise Allen/flickr.com (CC BY-SA 2.0). **Jacket Flaps:** © Photo: Takashi Ota/flickr.com (CC BY 2.0) (fireflies); © Marc Zimmer (axolotl).

ABOUT THE AUTHOR

Marc Zimmer is a professor of chemistry at Connecticut College. His research focuses on understanding and designing brighter fluorescent proteins. He has written two books about the green fluorescent protein, *Glowing Genes* and *Illuminating Disease*. He gives talks about fluorescent proteins around the world. His GFP website (http://www.conncoll.edu/ccacad/ zimmer/GFP-ww/GFP-1 .htm) has been highlighted in *Science* magazine and has had more than 1.8 million visitors.

As an expert on fluorescent proteins and their use in medical research, Zimmer has been quoted in *Nature, Science,* the *Scientist,* and the *Economist*. He has published articles in *USA Today*, the *LA Times*, the *Providence Journal*, and the *Hartford Courant*. In 2008 Zimmer briefed the Nobel Committee for Chemistry on fluorescent proteins and the scientists responsible for the GFP biotechnology revolution. He and his wife attended the Nobel Prize for Chemistry awards ceremony in Stockholm, Sweden.

In 2012 *The Huffington Post* listed Zimmer as one of the top college professors in the United States. At his college and as part of the University of Virginia's shipboard Semester at Sea study abroad program, Zimmer teaches classes about bioluminescence and its applications in medical research. Edgar, his GFP axolotl, accompanies Zimmer on field trips to talk about bioluminescence at schools.